Wellbeing for Sustainability in the Global Workplace

T0361954

Wellbeing in the workplace is an essential element in fostering a worker's sense of being valued, ensuring their engagement, and ultimately leading to higher levels of productivity and organizational performance. This important book specifically adds to the discussion by taking a global perspective, and evaluates wellbeing in the workplace in different countries, identifying both universal issues and specific cultural issues.

Chapter authors have been drawn from across five continents and eleven countries to provide ground-breaking research in wellbeing from different regional perspectives, looking at both developed and developing world scenarios. What is clear throughout the book is that organizations that are *not* people-centered undermine their capacity to attain and maintain quality standards, high performance, and competitiveness.

Organizational concerns about workers' wellbeing are growing exponentially due to the global VUCA (volatile, uncertain, complex, ambiguous) environment. In this environment, organizational success is no longer simply based on short-term revenue maximization, capital investments, or sales, but increasingly depends on people's wellbeing, human capital, and the development of human talent to ensure sustained and sustainable growth and performance. This book presents a collection of studies that address current and forthcoming organizational challenges and offer realistic solutions to support leaders and managers seeking to balance and value the contribution of people with long-term organizational performance.

Paola Ochoa is a Professor at the Graduate School of Management ESPAE, ESPOL, Ecuador.

Maria-Teresa Lepeley is the President and CEO at Global Institute for Quality Education. She has been a member of the Board of Examiners of the Baldridge National Quality Awards of the United States and adviser to National Quality Award Programs in Latin America.

Peter Essens is the Director of the Center of Expertise HRM & Organizational Behavior, Faculty of Economics and Business, University of Groningen, the Netherlands.

List of endorsements

'The topic of wellbeing at work has been discussed by many authors for a long time. Depending on the organizational context there are multiple approaches to studying wellbeing. One of the most relevant aspects is the relationship between worker's performance and physical and mental health. Congratulations to editors and authors for this brilliant work that explores wellbeing with broad and current approaches!'

Mario Teixeira Reis Neto, Professor,
Doctoral and Master Business Program, Fumec University, Brazil

'At a time when organizations face unavoidable disruptions it is essential a better and comprehensive understanding of wellbeing in the workplace. This book provides a collection of innovative perspectives from around the world to understand and implement solutions to improve the wellbeing of people.'

Jacobo Ramirez, Assistant Professor in Latin American Business
Development, Copenhagen Business School, Denmark

'The social construction of wellbeing at work is being challenged by new cohorts of workers whose values and priorities are shaped by historical social and economic global events quite different from previous generations. This book helps organizations understand those differences, how to build workplace environments and cultures that support these new generational paradigms and can include their best and brightest.'

Josephine McMurray, Assistant Professor,
Lazaridis School of Business & Economics,
Wilfrid Laurier University, Canada

'There are two important roles of management in society: to create innovations and new products that satisfy societal needs, and to manage and nurture healthy organizations that promote the wellbeing of collaborators. This book is a very timely and solid contribution to this discussion, both for educators and decision makers.'

Sergio Olavarrieta, Vice-Dean of the Faculty of Economics
and Business, University of Chile, Chile

'This is an apt title to put forth in the current business environment as it entails a primordial perspective often neglected in performance management: Management is always about people and success in any kind of undertakings relies on how people feel about conditions in their workplace. Institutions prosper if they provide not just an atmosphere but real circumstances for wellbeing from the shop floor to the C-suites. The great benefit of this book is the wide array of viewpoints on wellbeing in the workplace.'

Roland Bardy, Board Member,
Wittenberg Center for Global Ethics, Germany

'The downward cycle of being over-extended and exhausted negatively affects the organisational culture. These cycles can lead to burnout for individuals and slow death for organizations. This book analyzes one of the most worrying and essential matters of our current society: wellbeing at work. From an innovative and practical perspective, it is a crucial book for organisations genuinely interested in understanding wellbeing in the workplace and the main issues and challenges impacting it.'

Jorge Colvin, Associate Professor, Department of Finance, Faculty of Economics and Business, The Schiller International University, USA

'This compilation of chapters on well-being is very timely as workplace stress increases with the pressure to compete. I found the book very informative and well written.'

Joyeeta Gupta, Professor of Environment and Development in the Global South, University of Amsterdam, The Netherlands

'In a world where the conditions and contexts of business models globally are continually changing and adapting, it is important to remember the foundations and pillars of organizations. Since wellbeing in the workplace is one of the most important, this book helps to understand its essence and dimensions through an exciting and relevant collection of intellectual contributions.'

Raúl Montalvo, Director, EGADE Business School in Guadalajara, Tecnologico de Monterrey, Mexico

'This book will be useful to those who are looking for innovative ways of understanding and managing human wellbeing in organizations. It is an important contribution to comparative thinking, drawing from multiple national experiences.'

Jose Joaquín Brunner, UNESCO Chair, Comparative Higher Education Systems and Policies, Universidad Diego Portales, Chile

'For the last 80 years, scientists have been highly aware of the importance to synchronize technical with social change. Nonetheless, financial-economic per-formance goals frequently have superseded social goals in most management approaches. This book on human centered management and employee wellbeing resonates as a new management framework enhancing attention on the role of human beings in company's success. The alignment shown in this book converging human minded workers with high performance work systems in the workplace brings about necessary innovation in the twenty-first century.'

Peter Oeij, Senior Research Scientist, The Netherlands Organisation, The Netherlands

'Wellbeing at work is an imperative rising to the top of the agenda of company managers, policy makers and stakeholders. The workplace is, besides providing a living, also about a positive environment to develop oneself and to find meaningful relations with others. This book shows how to understand the emerging concept of human wellbeing in the workplace. It shows that wellbeing at work is no longer a luxury of Western workers but a priority worldwide. The book shows and shares experiences from around the world on wellbeing at work. Practitioners and researchers will find good reasons to invest time in this important subject.'

Steven Dhondt, Professor in Sociological Research,
University of Leuven, Belgium

'The effects of economic globalization have produced negative effects on the health of workers with major managerial challenge for organizations. Social development and economic growth are sustainable when they are synchronized with the promotion of wellbeing at work. The global effects are even more perverse in countries like Brazil where organizations are less inclined to make investments in strategies and structures that promote wellbeing at work. This book includes relevant international contributions from a variety of countries about organizational changes focused on effective management of wellbeing at work. I highly endorse its publication.'

Jairo Eduardo Borges-Andrade, Professor, Graduate Program
in Social, Work and Organizational Psychology,
University of Brasília, Brazil

'Nurturing wellbeing of individuals and organizations in a sustainable way is a major challenge of Industry 4.0. Wellbeing is a major indicator of quality of life, health, adjustment, and thriving. This book breaks new ground by bringing wellbeing to the forefront on a sustainable and global basis.'

Nicholas Beutell, Professor of Management,
School of Business, Iona College, USA

'The amount of challenges and disruptions the workforce and managers are facing are unprecedented in modern history. Demographic change, competing global markets, economic uncertainty, new technology, all defy the most important dimension of the workplace: people. Organizational mission and the wellbeing of people present significant challenges to balance, but in the last century the metrics of success has been skewed towards financial outcomes often at the expense of people and wellbeing. This book explores a comprehensive number of paths to success centered on people across many dimensions of wellbeing, from safety to job satisfaction, from education to achieving self-actualization. A certainly welcome new vision of wellbeing in the workplace!'

Ronald W. Tarr, former Senior Research Faculty Member
& Lab Director (ret), Institute for Simulation and Training,
University of Central Florida, USA

'This timely book on well-being for sustainability is true to its title providing global perspectives on this topic. The well-researched chapters offer a diversity of perspectives, including psychological, sociological and labor market insights, together with a critical look at issues of talent management, gender, millennial and generational issues, health and safety, cross-cultural and comparative international perspectives including those from emerging markets. The editors and chapter authors are to be commended for an insightful work which will be of great benefit to scholars and practitioners alike.'

Frank M. Horwitz, Cranfield School of Management,
Cranfield University, UK

'Refreshingly practical yet profoundly insightful, this book on wellbeing crafts a must-read leadership and people development guide for managers who are working at the coal-face to engage, retain, and capitalise on the potential of every nation's rich and diverse talent.'

Candida Schoerger, HR Business Partner, DXC Technology,
South Africa

Human Centered Management

The purpose of the book series is to re-position people to be at the center of organizations, the economy and society. Using management as the common denominator, the ultimate goal is to perform a paradigm shift from the entrenched approaches of the industrial past to a human-centered methodology which is convergent with the needs of people and organizations in the constantly changing interconnected world that frames the new Knowledge Society.

The challenges that management is facing when dealing with human development, active participation, responsible leadership, financial accountability, and social responsibility issues can only be understood and solved through the cross-fertilization of ideas from different disciplines. Better integration between management, psychology, neuroscience, economics, education, business, and others, needs to happen to accrue the benefits. The reason is simple. Global conditions create increasingly complex problems that can be highly disruptive. Solutions require approaches that build resilience through embedding multidisciplinary models that are effective in building productive organizations, transparent markets, sustainable economies and inclusive societies.

Maria-Teresa Lepeley, Principal Editor
Maria-Teresa is an educator and economist. After a career in academia, she founded the Global Institute for Quality Education (GIQE) to respond to the challenges in achieving sustainable quality. She designs GIQE's programs and projects and delivers them worldwide, connecting networks of sustainable quality innovators and problem solvers.

Roland Bardy, Associate Editor
Roland Bardy is Executive Professor of General Management and Leadership at Florida Gulf Coast University, USA. He is also owner of BardyConsult in Mannheim, Germany.

Human Centered Management
5 Pillars of Organizational Quality and Global Sustainability
Maria-Teresa Lepeley

Rethinking Leadership
A Human-Centered Approach to Management Ethics
Roland Bardy

Wellbeing for Sustainability in the Global Workplace
Edited by Paola Ochoa, Maria-Teresa Lepeley, Peter Essens

https://www.routledge.com/Human-Centered-Management/book-series/HUMCM

Wellbeing for Sustainability in the Global Workplace

Edited by
Paola Ochoa, Maria-Teresa
Lepeley, and Peter Essens

Routledge
Taylor & Francis Group

LONDON AND NEW YORK

First published 2019 by Routledge

2 Park Square, Milton Park, Abingdon, Oxon, OX14 4RN
605 Third Avenue, New York, NY 10017

Routledge is an imprint of the Taylor & Francis Group, an informa business

First issued in paperback 2020

British Library Cataloguing-in-Publication Data
A catalogue record for this book is available from the British Library

Library of Congress Cataloging-in-Publication Data
A catalog record has been requested for this book

ISBN: 978-1-138-60089-8 (hbk)
ISBN: 978-0-367-73419-0 (pbk)

Typeset in Times New Roman
by Florence Production Ltd, Stoodleigh, Devon, UK

Contents

Figures

Tables

About the editors

Paola Ochoa Pacheco

Escuela Superior Politécnica del Litoral,
ESPOL, ESPAE Graduate School of
Management
Ecuador
pjochoa@espol.edu.ec

PhD Social Psychology, Autonomous University
of Barcelona, Spain. Led Human Resources
Division in petroleum company in Venezuela and
has advanced academic career in Venezuela,
Ecuador and Spain. Professor at Escuela Superior
Politécnica del Litoral, ESPOL, ESPAE Graduate
School of Management, Ecuador. Research: wellbeing, psychosocial risks at work, values and
meaning of working. Advisor in Human Resources
and Organizational Behavior.

Maria-Teresa Lepeley

President, Global Institute for Quality Education
United States
mtlepeley@globalqualityeducation.org

President and founder of the Global Institute for Quality Education. Economist, educator, entrepreneur. Has directed executive programs in the University of Connecticut, USA, and at School of Business, Universidad de Chile. Author and editor of the Human Centered Management Book Series (Routledge) and Innovation in Human Centered Sustainability Book Series. International speaker in Sustainable Quality. Former Examiners of US Baldrige National Quality Award and adviser to NQA programs in six countries in Latin America. Her previous book in the HCM Series is *Human Centered Management: 5 Pillars of Organizational Quality and Global Sustainability* (2017, Routledge).

Peter Essens

Department of HRM & Organizational
Behavior, Faculty of Economics and Business,
University of Groningen
Groningen, the Netherlands
p.j.m.d.essens@rug.nl

Director Center of Expertise of HRM and Organizational Behavior, Faculty of Economics and Business, University of Groningen, the Netherlands. Principal Scientist, Human and Organizational Innovations at Netherlands Applied Scientific Research institute TNO. PhD Social Sciences. Research: how people work, organize, and collaborate to master complex problems in settings with multiple actors in business and in civil and military security and safety settings.

Contributing authors

Daniela M. Andrei

University of Western Australia, Business School
Australia
daniela.andrei@uwa.edu.au

Daniela Andrei is a Research Fellow at the Business School, University of Western Australia, working across two world class research centers: Centre for Safety (C4S) and Centre for Transformative Work Design. Daniela completed her PhD in Psychology at Babes-Bolyai University in Romania in 2010. In 2012, after being awarded the competitive GO8 European Fellowship, she joined UWA, where she continued as a Research Fellow. Her current research activities revolve around safety, team leadership and team processes/emergent states and effectiveness of incident command teams in oil and gas industry as well as work design and antecedents of work design decisions.

Josep M. Blanch

Professor Emeritus at the Autonomous University of Barcelona, Spain
Professor at the San Buenaventura University, Cali, Colombia
josepmaria.blanch@uab.cat
jmblanchr@usbcali.edu.co

Josep M. Blanch is PhD in Psychology and Graduated in Social Sciences. He is currently Professor Emeritus at the Autonomous University of Barcelona and Professor at the San Buenaventura University, Cali, Colombia. As an academic and research fellow, he has been invited by several dozen Latin American, Spanish and European universities. He has also been consultant to government agencies in Catalan, Spanish, European and Latin American contexts, and coordinator of international research teams. He is the author of numerous books, articles, chapters and technical reports on quality of working life, occupational health and psycho-social risks at work.

Anabela Correia

Polytechnic Institute of Setúbal & GOVCOPP
Portugal
anabela.correia@esce.ips.pt

Anabela Correia has a PhD in Social and Organizational Psychology from the University of Salamanca (Spain). She is a Coordinator Professor of the School of Business Sciences of the Polytechnic Institute of Setubal and Leader of the Human Resource Management Degree of this Institution. She is a researcher at the Competitiveness, Governance and Public Policy (GOVCOPP) research unit at the University of Aveiro, Portugal. She has published articles in international journals, presented several communications in national and international conferences and her main research interests cover people management, organizational behavior and the quality of working life.

Mário César Ferreira

Department of Social Psychology and Work Psychology, Institute of the University of Brasilia (UNB)
Brazil
ferreiramariocesar@gmail.com

Occupational Psychologist, PhD from Ecole Pratique des Hautes Etudes (EPHE, France), postdoctoral research in Occupational Ergonomics Applied to Quality of Work Life at Université Paris, Sorbonne (France). Associate Professor, Department and the Graduate Program of Social and Occupational Psychology at the Institute of Psychology - University of Brasilia (UnB). Ad-hoc consultant: CNPq (Brazilian National Research Council), CAPES (Coordination for Higher Education Staff Development), publications in scientific journals in health and occupational sciences. Author and coordinator of books, chapters, articles, chapters and technical reports on quality of working life, occupational health published in Brazil. Coordinator of CNPq's Research Groups 'Staff Development, Quality of Work Life and Learning in the Public Sector (DViTra)'.

Mark A. Griffin

University of Western Australia, Business School
Australia
mark.griffin@uwa.edu.au

Mark Griffin is a Professor of Management at the University of Western Australia. He received his PhD from the Pennsylvania State University, USA, and is currently Associate Editor for the *Journal of Applied Psychology* and is past Associate Editor of the *Journal of Management*. Mark's research examines the way individuals contribute to organizational performance and he has managed large-scale organizational studies in areas of safety, leadership, wellbeing, and productivity. He has developed assessment tools for use in a range of industries across Australia, Europe, UK, USA and Asia.

Kety Jáuregui

ESAN University, Graduate School of Business
Peru
kjauregui@esan.edu.pe

PhD in Management at IESE, Spain. She is Professor of Administration at ESAN University, Peru. Her research interests include corporate responsibility and human resource management. She is Director of the Master in People Organization and Management at ESAN University. She is also invited Professor at University ESPAE-ESPOL, Ecuador, and at the Management faculty in University Externado, Colombia. She received a Bachelor's degree in Industrial Engineering at UNI, Perú and a Masters of Administration degree from the ITESM, Mexico.

Nicky Pouw

University of Amsterdam
The Netherlands
N.R.N.Pouw@uva.nl

Nicky Pouw is as an economist and Associate Professor at the Governance and Inclusive Development group at the University of Amsterdam, the Netherlands. She has over twenty years of research experience on inclusive development, poverty, inequality, gender and the economics of wellbeing, mostly in Africa. She is co-editor of the book (with Isa Baud) *Local Governance and Poverty in Developing Nations* (2012, Routledge) and author of the monograph Introduction to Gender and Wellbeing in Microeconomics (2017, Routledge). Currently, she manages three international research programs on: Social Protection in Ghana and Kenya; Women Food Entrepreneurship in Burkina Faso and Kenya; and Social Exclusion of Vulnerable Youth in six countries. She has published two special issues on Inclusive Development, one for the *European Journal of Development Research* (2015) and one for the *COSUST Journal* (2016). She is a member of the scientific Board of the African Study Centre, Leiden University and visiting lecturer at UNESCO-IHE Delft University.

Linda Ronnie

University of Cape Town, Graduate School of Business
South Africa
linda.ronnie@gsb.uct.ac.za

Dr Linda Ronnie is Associate Professor in Organisational Behaviour and People Management at the University of Cape Town's Graduate School of Business in South Africa. Her teaching focuses on a wide range of people management topics, including organizational culture, motivation, teamwork, labor relations and managing change. Linda's research interests include talent management in diverse contexts, exploring the psychological contract, and examining management pedagogy. A committed management educator, Linda was presented with the prestigious UCT Distinguished Teacher's Award in 2014 and is the award-winning co-author of the Best 2015 Emerald Emerging Markets Case Study, both firsts for the UCT GSB.

José Manuel Saiz-Alvarez

EGADE Business School, Tecnológico de Monterrey
Mexico
jmsaiz@itesm.mx

PhD Economics and Business Administration, Autonomous University of Madrid (Spain) and PhD Political Science and Sociology, Pontifical University of Salamanca (Spain). Postdoctoral studies in the USA, Estonia and Spain. Research Professor, EGADE Business School-Tecnológico de Monterrey (Mexico). Visiting Professor, the Catholic University of Santiago de Guayaquil (Ecuador), and St Francis Xavier University of Chuquisaca (Bolivia). More than 200 publications of international prestige. Scientific committees' member of indexed journals in Europe, America and Asia.

Preface

The wellbeing of people has been a main concern for humankind. For Greek philosophers in BC times human wellbeing was a central matter for progress and a fundamental drive for society. And their thoughts have influenced conceptions of wellbeing from then until today.

But in the twentieth century the importance of human wellbeing was displaced by the pressing imperatives of the first industrial revolution, enhancing machines and processes in a period of deep change and transformation with significant impact on societies, economies, and people. Nobody doubts the benefits of the industrial past and the extraordinary progress that improved the lives of people advancing societies to the remarkable world we have today – remarkable in comparison with life in pre-industrial societies, and in terms of giving people access to water, food, electricity, cars, and roads that substantially diminish physical distances. But history shows that industrial pursuits and material progress are only part of the equation and, to a large extent, a focus on human wellbeing in the workforce cannot be a marginal subject and has ample space for improvement.

During this millennium, concern for wellbeing has gained increasing attention in the workplace, in management, economics, and business sciences, and these disciplines are turning to psychology, health care, philosophy, ethics, and new developments in neuroscience, to understand more and to learn how to improve and consolidate human wellbeing in synchrony with organizational wellbeing.

The importance of wellbeing in the workplace is a significant challenge for organizations in the global VUCA (volatile, uncertain, complex, ambiguous) environment, which face unavoidable disruptions that neither the best organizational structures nor the finest strategies are able to easily solve. For organizations to survive and thrive, the creativity, adaptability, and engagement of the people who work in the organization is essential. And their wellbeing is center stage.

The 12 authors of the ten chapters in the book, representing countries in North and Latin America, Europe, Australia, and Africa, provide a balanced global view of developed and developing countries. Their diverse fields and experiences offer leaders, managers, and employees options to find the shortest possible road to continuous improvement in leading and wellbeing in organizations.

We understand wellbeing challenges in management and the workplace as a human imperative highly correlated with critical elements that drive gender equality, organizational performance, productivity, competitiveness, and sustainability. These concerns are aligned with global challenges in the workplace pursued by EUROSTAT, the European Foundation for the Improvement of Working and Living Conditions (EUROFUND), the International Labour Organization (ILO), the Centre d'études de l'emploi, and many other organizations focused on wellbeing in the workplace and the impact of psycho-emotional, social, and economic variables.

Gallup organization's 2017 State of the Global Workplace reports that only 17 percent of employees in organizations in 155 countries feel engaged with their work and thriving; the rest are struggling or suffering. The high percentage of workers disengaged with the work they perform on a daily basis shows the dimension of the problem and the surmounting obstacles organizations face to improve the wellbeing of people to attain sustainability.

The book is divided in three parts:

- Part I **Understanding Wellbeing** focuses on identification of different frameworks to assess wellbeing in the workplace.
- Part II **Wellbeing and work** discusses the main issues and challenges impacting wellbeing.
- Part III **Emerging Wellbeing Forms** discusses experiences in different sectors in countries around the world with a new focus on wellbeing.

The editors commend the efforts and audacity of chapter authors to explore in the emerging field of wellbeing in management and appreciate their interest to pioneer solutions. We would also like to thank David Coello, research assistant at ESPAE Graduate School of Management, who helped a great deal preparing the manuscript and the index. We deeply thank a large number of colleagues, family, and friends around the world, who have inspired us to undertake this human-centered challenge and endeavor. We hope that all our readers enjoy and benefit from this human journey.

PO   MTL   PE

Part I
Understanding wellbeing

1 Psychosocial wellbeing at work

Reasons to invest in healthy employees and workplaces

Paola Ochoa and Josep M. Blanch

Introduction

Throughout the twentieth century, the psychology of work focused its research and intervention in the analysis and prevention of labor malaise. In contrast, the psychology of the organization did not have that negativist bias. In general, however, organizational studies focused on wellbeing and job satisfaction as something associated with and subordinate to some processes that were considered more central, such as performance, productivity, efficiency, quality, competitiveness, culture, climate, and development.

From the twenty-first century, driven by the current of *Positive Psychology*, research on work and organizational processes has analyzed the optimal functioning of people and teams within organizations, the development of healthy workplaces and organizations, and the reciprocal influence between organizational dynamics and staff wellbeing. In this respect, numerous studies provide growing evidence that work wellbeing generates positive impacts on organizational outcomes such as job performance, competitiveness, quality standards, and sustainability (Bakker & Schaufeli, 2008; Bakker *et al.*, 2008; Bakker & Leiter, 2010; Clark & Senik, 2014; De Neve *et al.*, 2013; EU-OSHA, 2014; Grawitch & Ballard, 2016; Luthans, Avolio, Avey, & Norman, 2007; Luthans, Youssef, & Avolio, 2007; Rodríguez-Carvajal, Moreno-Jiménez, Rivas-Hermosilla, Álvarez-Bejarano, & Sanz Vergel, 2010; Schulte & Vainio, 2010; WHO, 2010, 2017; Youssef & Luthans, 2010). From these findings are derived some requirements concerning human talent management, the prevention of psychosocial risks, promotion of happiness at work, and improvement of healthy work environments.

In this context, it makes sense to ask what conceptions of wellbeing at work are handled by the literature and how the financial and psychosocial aspects of work wellbeing are articulated in such constructs. According to the interdisciplinary consensus, the relationship between financial and psychosocial work wellbeing does not follow a linear model. Once basic needs are satisfied, increases in wellbeing appear linked not to financial but to psychosocial factors associated with personal development, quality of working life, occupational health, and opportunities for experiencing positive self-referential cognitions and emotions (Bakker & Leiter, 2010; Granero, Blanch, & Ochoa, 2017; Luthans, Avolio, Avey, & Norman, 2007).

The aim of this chapter is to integrate interdisciplinary constructions on work wellbeing, focusing on its positive consequences for employees, organizations, and society.

Working, living, and wellbeing

Work is a way of relating to things we produce and use and to people with whom we interact, collaborating or exchanging goods, products, or services. Omnipresent throughout history and across cultures, it consumes all kinds of energies, thoughts, emotions, efforts, and times in the lives of most people in all societies. The quality of our lives is marked by our experience of work as a source of wellbeing but also malaise, blessings and curses, emancipation and alienation, and success and failure, of healthy effects and pathological consequences. Each society configures a predominant vision of work, referring to rights and responsibilities, prescriptions and proscriptions, imperatives and taboos.

For most people, work is the principal way to obtain earnings necessary for personal survival and that of their families and communities. This instrumental function has made it a powerful motivational factor. However, scientific literature of the last century has provided empirical evidence that labor activity constitutes not only a means of earning money by way of salary but also a standard way of developing subjectivity at personal, social, and cultural levels. For this reason, formal employment consumes a large proportion of the daily life of people and families in cities and nations, functioning as basic support for social order and integration and a determinant of physical and mental health, wellbeing, and quality of life. From most diverse disciplines, work is considered a human activity that transcends the simple instinctive response to the biological imperative of material survival, making it unique for its reflexive, conscious, propositional, strategic, instrumental, social, and moral nature. According to this perspective (Blanch, 2012), the work environment contributes to the development of psychological experiences of positive signs, such as health and wellbeing, satisfaction and happiness, certainty and safety, achievement and realization, recognition and identity, and self-referential cognitions and emotions such as autonomy, self-expression, self-efficacy, and self-esteem. On the other hand, work can generate negative emotions such as discomfort, anxiety, distress, depression, emotional exhaustion, feelings of ineffectiveness, frustration, hopelessness, and helplessness.

The work–wellbeing relationship can be described as the chronicle of a fundamental ambivalence; work wellbeing refers to the rewarding and successful experience of doing, with effort and purpose, something economically, socially, and personally productive. However, it also refers to the experience of discomfort associated with work risk, failure, or frustration.

The literature provides evidence that the degree of physical, psychological, and social wellbeing work provides to working people depends on two factors: working conditions and subjective conceptions of work that dominate in time and place (Ardichvili & Kuchinke, 2009; Granero *et al.*, 2017; Ochoa & Blanch, 2016). Working conditions are a set of ecological, material, technical, economic, social, political, legal, and organizational circumstances and characteristics within which labor activity and relationships are developed. This context has a direct impact on the quality of work, on health and safety, motivation and commitment, satisfaction and discomfort, work performance, and occupational pathologies. It also has decisive influence on the dynamics of organizations in two senses: positively, on productivity and competitiveness, efficiency and effectiveness, excellence and sustainability; and negatively, on conflict, absenteeism and presentism, turnover, desertion of the job or profession, accidents, or occupational diseases (Blanch, Sahagún & Cervantes, 2010). Conceptions of work derive from historical and cultural backgrounds of working practice. They express the way each society understands, interprets, values, and constructs through language and common sense its particular vision of the working experience. In this respect, throughout history and cultures, work has been experienced and narrated as a factor of wellbeing and as a source of discontent. Each culture shapes a dominant version of what work entails as blessing or curse, of healthy experience or pathology.

Then, why do people work? Sustenance or accomplishment

Are we working for immediate salary rewards or to fulfill a job mission in life? What motivates us more to work? What we can do or buy with money obtained from employment; the personal, professional, social, or family goals attained from work; or all these reasons at the same time? If the latter, how do workers rank these motives and values? What can explain that, in recent decades, a majority of people across continents and cultures, genres and generations, state preference to continue working even if they should win a lottery that would solve all economic needs for the rest of their lives?

Ryan and Deci (2001) asked the question, *To be happy or to be self-fulfilled,* and Huta and Ryan (2010) wondered whether people are *Pursuing pleasure or virtue*. Both statements reflect the current situation in a debate that goes throughout Western history. One of the first axes of philosophical discussion on the nature of happiness and its paths goes back to Greek classics in the fourth century BC, establishing tensions between eudemonist and hedonist views. Epicurus of Samos represents the hedonistic approach, defending the human capacity to choose, in a free, rational, and prudent way, a vital pursuit of pleasure and avoidance of pain while at the same time avoiding the extremes of renunciation and self-indulgence. Epicureanism affirmed the superiority of the pleasures of the soul (deep and durable) over those of the body (superficial and ephemeral). In contrast, according to Aristotle as the representative of eudemonism, all human action points to an end, and the ultimate goal of ethics is happiness. This final state must be sought with rationality, more strictly related to virtue than to pleasure.

Both traditions point to happiness as the ideal state of human existence and assume as morally good the paths leading to happiness. At this point, the differences between these orientations are evident: on the one hand, the radical version of the hedonistic tradition proclaims as good everything that leads to pleasure and as evil what generates pain. From this perspective, wellbeing is the state that allows one to access pleasure and avoid pain. On the other hand, the eudemonist perspective emphasizes the achievement of goals as a *sine qua non-*condition for happiness. In the contemporary scientific literature, both tendencies are outlined.

The central construct of the hedonistic approach is that subjective wellbeing includes three components: an assessment of satisfaction with life, the presence of positive emotions, and the absence of negative emotions (Cameron & Spreitzer, 2011; De Neve *et al.*, 2013; EUROSTAT, 2016; OECD, 2013). Hedonic wellbeing consists of a set of value judgments and emotional reactions regarding the degree of satisfaction with one's own life in general or in relevant aspects such as health, family, and work. The OECD (2013) *Guidelines on Measuring Subjective Wellbeing* states that determinants of wellbeing go beyond people's income and material conditions.

Eudemonistic psychological wellbeing includes a question about life meaning and purpose. Ryff developed a model in which the central axis is the development of human potential (Ryff & Singer, 2008). It includes six dimensions: self-acceptance, positive relationships with people, personal autonomy, mastery of the environment, purpose in life, and personal growth. This conception of wellbeing appears associated with the classic ideal of good living as good work and the philosophical triple aspiration to the ethical realization of goodness, aesthetic enjoyment of beauty, and epistemic production of truth.

Despite this differentiation, there are numerous attempts to establish bridges between the two traditions (Deci & Ryan, 2008; Díaz, Blanco, & Durán, 2011; Huta & Ryan, 2010; Kashdan, Biswas-Diener, & King, 2008; Robertson & Cooper, 2011). According to Díaz, Stavraki, Blanco, and Gandarillas (2015), satisfaction with life is not strictly a hedonic concept because it contains many eudemonic components. In addition, neither pleasure nor goals are achieved in a vacuum but in a context in which social and personal variables are combined. For this reason, this point of view calls for greater integration of hedonic and eudemonic traditions, proposing a synthetic model of wellbeing composed of satisfaction with life and achievement of vital goals.

In this line, Robertson and Cooper (2011) propose a model of Occupational Psychological Wellbeing that embraces a double psychological scope – affective and propositional – in which happiness appears as a synthesis of personal satisfaction and personal growth. According to Kashdan, Biswas-Diener, and King (2008), an integrated concept of happiness integrates pleasure, satisfaction with life, virtuous practice, and achievement of relevant goals. Work wellbeing consists of a psychosocial state of cognitive and emotional joyful living, leading to the ability to successfully and flexibly interrelate job responsibilities with personal and professional competences, resources, and organizational demands. Aiming in this direction, the World Health Organization (WHO) defines a Healthy Workplace as one that facilitates access to physical, psychological, and social wellbeing experiences for people in a work environment that enables them to develop their projects and achieve work goals (WHO, 2010, 2017).

Benefits of work wellbeing

The complex and intense relationships between work and wellbeing have traditionally been studied by work and organizational scientists, taking as reference the conventional medical view of occupational health: a reactive approach aimed at the resolution or handling of problems based on mitigating or eliminating negative effects. This has led to a marked pathological bias in the study of wellbeing at work, which has been scored as labor malaise. Schaufeli and Bakker (2004) criticize that, throughout the twentieth century, psychological research on negative aspects of work experience (focusing on "symptoms" of distress, burnout, anxiety, depression, minor mental disorders, psychophysiological dysfunctions) dominated with a ratio of 15 to 1 over positive dimensions such as happiness, satisfaction, wellbeing, and self-realization. However, the turn of the twenty-first century opens the way to global approaches that assess negative and positive poles of health and wellbeing at work.

In the study on work wellbeing, the initial emphasis on economic dimension and physical, material, and technological ecology has shifted towards the psychosocial and organizational aspects of work. Similarly, wage hedonism increasingly coexists with the eudemonic search for expressive and meaningful elements of work. People do not work only for money but also for many non-salary compensations, such as good working conditions, safety and health at work, job stability, growth opportunities, career prospects, recognition by the organization, positive social climate or autonomy, and participation in professional decision-making (Bakker & Schaufeli, 2008; Bakker *et al.*, 2008; Blanch, Sahagún, Cantera & Cervantes, 2010; Goulart, Blanch, Sahagún & Bobsin, 2012; Granero *et al.*, 2017; Ochoa & Blanch, 2016; Warr, 2007).

Moreover, other series of transitions contribute to modifying the work scene. The traditional emphasis on physical, technical, ergonomic, hygienic, and mechanical aspects of working conditions opens the way to the psychosocial and subjective dimensions of labor experience and relations. Recognition of the relevance of psychosocial risk factors at work has much to do with transformations in organizations and management with health, safety, and wellbeing risks promoted by the International Labor Organization (ILO, 2012), WHO (2010, 2017), and European Agency for Safety and Health at Work (EU OSHA, 2013, 2014, 2015).

The emphasis on evaluation of economic costs of accidents, occupational pathologies, and dysfunctional behaviors for companies and countries, such as absenteeism, evolved towards the prevention of all occupational hazards and especially psychosocial risks, emphasizing the promotion of wellbeing, occupational health, and healthy organizations. To this end, new proposals of global organizations, such as the Healthy Workplaces proposed by the WHO (2010), conceived as a model for action for employers, workers, policymakers, and practitioners, have made a significant contribution. This ideal work environment is "one in which managers and workers collaborate to attain continual process improvement to protect and promote health, safety and wellbeing of all workers and sustainability of the workplace," considering health and safety concerns in the physical and psychosocial work environment, including the organization of work and workplace culture. The foundational program of this global organization (1948) defined health as "a state of complete physical, mental, and social well-being." The WHO (2017) proposed "improving the wellbeing of the population" as a political priority and the evaluation of this wellbeing as a strategic component for organizations (see Table 1.1).

On a more general level, in 2011, the General Assembly of the United Nations invited member countries to evaluate happiness in their populations as an element to guide public policies and to assess the progress of nations around the world. This initiative generated the *World Happiness Report* series, produced by a multidisciplinary team of leading experts across fields including economics, psychology, survey analysis, national statistics, public policy, and health. The editors of recent reports argue that measures of wellbeing provide a better indicator of quality of life than income, poverty, education, or health analyzed separately. In the same way, they consider wellbeing as a broader and more accurate measurement of human progress. World Happiness Reports include rankings of wellbeing within and between countries. At a theoretical level, this kind of report underlines the political importance of happiness, because the levels of subjective wellbeing predict the future of health, productivity, and wealth (United Nations, 2015, 2016). The OECD (2013, 2015) proposed its own guidelines to measure subjective wellbeing. Along the same lines, the EU OSHA (2014, 2015) launched the campaign that *Good Safety and Health at Work Is Good Business,* and the European Commission (2012) itself set the goal of wellbeing as a new priority for Europe's health policy towards the 2020 horizon with the slogan *Investing in wellbeing at work.*

Table 1.1 Benefits of Workplace Health Promotion.

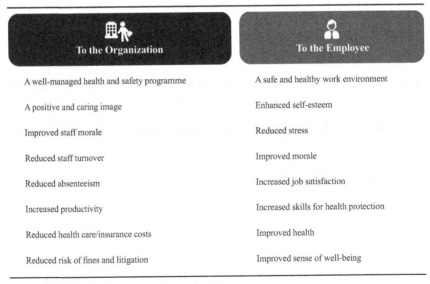

To the Organization	To the Employee
A well-managed health and safety programme	A safe and healthy work environment
A positive and caring image	Enhanced self-esteem
Improved staff morale	Reduced stress
Reduced staff turnover	Improved morale
Reduced absenteeism	Increased job satisfaction
Increased productivity	Increased skills for health protection
Reduced health care/insurance costs	Improved health
Reduced risk of fines and litigation	Improved sense of well-being

Source: World Health Organization (www.who.int).

In economic, social, and political sciences, there is also a rise in studies on subjective and psychological wellbeing (Choi & Chentsova-Dutton, 2016; Clark & Senik, 2014; Diener, Helliwell & Kahneman, 2010; Helliwell, Huang, & Wang, 2014; Helliwell & Putnam, 2005; Layard, 2011; McMahon, 2006). Such a phenomenon is equally impressive in psychological scientific literature where the main research trend comes from the movement of "positive psychology" (Bakker & Schaufeli, 2008; Rodríguez-Carvajal *et al.*, 2010). Its application to the work and organizational field focuses on the human strengths that can be measured, developed, and managed to improve work performance (Luthans, Avolio, Avey & Norman, 2007; Luthans, Youssef & Avolio, 2007).

Positive organizational psychology seeks and finds relationships between job wellbeing and positive organizational results. In their review of 154 research articles on the subject, Rodríguez-Carvajal *et al.* (2010) conclude that organizational practices that favor the development and growth of employees lead to desirable results in performance that benefit the organization. In the same way, Luthans *et al.* (2007) argue that the opportunities offered by companies for the development of positive psychological capital aim to improve staff productivity. In sum, these studies conceive job wellbeing as the process and product of virtuous encounter between "positive employees" and "positive organizational results."

Among the positive individual factors is *Positive Psychological Capital*, a healthy state of individual development of which Luthans *et al.* (2007) and Youssef and Luthans (2010) emphasize the following characteristics: self-efficacy (confidence in one's own ability to make positive attributions to present and future success), hope (achieving goals and strategic initiatives to achieve them), optimism (expectation of the occurrence of positive events), and resilience (ability to successfully handle adversities and difficulties on way to achieve goals). Bakker and Leiter (2010) added engagement, a state of psychological attachment to work as a positive affective state of fullness characterized by vigor, dedication, and absorption or concentration at work.

Healthy working environments belong to the category of positive organizational factors in terms of social climate and contractual, temporary, and wage conditions of work; organizational and management models; material resources and design of workplaces; profile of competencies, career plans, opportunities for growth and promotion; autonomy; participation; and adequacy of available resources to existing labor demands.

Work wellbeing experienced by positive employees in positive organizations integrates multiple aspects: quality of working lives; occupational safety and health; and work meaning, goals, and sense. It has become a significant determinant of productivity and competitiveness at the individual, organizational, and societal levels (Figure 1.1).

One of the pillars in new models of management, and particularly in the 'Employees' Wellbeing in Sustainable Models' (Lepeley, 2017), is that health and wellbeing are important components of quality standards in organizations.

In summary, the study of and intervention in healthy workplaces from the psychological perspective focused on the complex relationship between employee

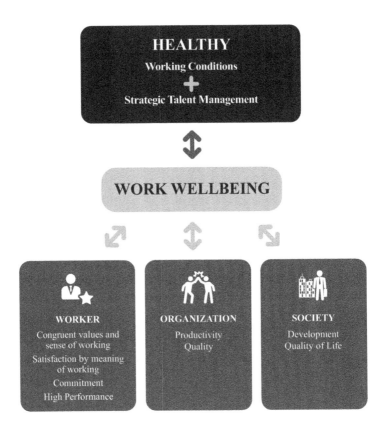

Figure 1.1 Antecedents and consequences of work wellbeing.
Source: Authors.

and organizational outcomes (Grawitch & Ballard, 2016). In the same way, the EU-OSHA (2013) conceived of wellbeing as "a summative concept that characterizes the quality of working lives, including occupational safety and health aspects." According to this point of view, work wellbeing "may be a major determinant of productivity at the individual, enterprise and societal levels." This report informs that different European countries and organizations converge in conceiving work wellbeing as a complex combination of job satisfaction, good working conditions, quality of working environment, and health at work.

Throughout the last decade, the American Psychological Association has been developing a *Psychologically Healthy Workplace Program* linking workers' wellbeing and organizational performance. The central axis of this program includes five key areas: employee involvement (creativity, autonomy, and participation in organizational decision-making), work–life balance (in flexible working time), employee growth and development (career plans, competence training), and healthy and safe work environments (prevention of psychosocial risks at work and promotion of work health and wellbeing).

Wellbeing and the road ahead

Work wellbeing is a relevant topic for organizational improvement. The archaic thesis that relationships between management and personnel followed rules of a zero-sum game, where one party wins all while the other party loses all, is going to be displaced by growing evidence that both parties can win (and can lose) on the side of the economic objective as well as subjective wellbeing. Indeed, there is a growing interdisciplinary consensus around the following propositions:

1. The levels of subjective wellbeing predict the future of workers' health and organizational competitiveness, productivity, and wealth. Marta Neira, Director of the WHO's Department of Public Health and Environment, argues, "The wealth of companies depends on the health of their workers" (WHO, 2010).
2. Managerial practices that favor employee development and growth lead to beneficial outcomes for the organization in the form of increased work performance.
3. Unsatisfied workers are bad business, but investing in healthy workplaces is good business for the organization, because it facilitates achievement of organizational objectives, prevents psychosocial risks, and promotes wellbeing of people in the organization. According to the EU OSHA (2014), Good Occupational Safety and Health is good for business, and good management of safety and health at work in a company is associated with improvement in performance and profitability.
4. Occupational wellbeing has political relevance, because it is interconnected with sustainable objectives of work and organization.
5. The growth of organizations requires design and development of tools and methods of work wellbeing evaluation.
6. Creating healthy work environments is a good policy to support the achievement of organizational objectives concerning the prevention of psychosocial risks and improving high performance and business goals.
7. Investing in work wellbeing is the best business for the company.
8. Work wellbeing must be linked to the culture, values, and management of any organization.

References

Ardichvili, A., & Kuchinke, K.P. (2009). International Perspectives on the Meanings of Work and Working: Current Research and Theory. *Advances in Developing Human Resources*, 11(2), 155–167.

Bakker, A.B., & Schaufeli, W.B. (Eds.) (2008). Special issue: Contexts of Positive Organizational Behavior. *Journal of Organizational Behavior*, 29 (2).

Bakker, A.B., Schaufeli, W.B., Leiter, M.P., & Taris, T.W. (Eds.) (2008). Special issue: Engagement at work. *Work & Stress*, 22(3), 185–294.

Bakker, A.B., & Leiter, M.P. (Eds.) (2010). *Work engagement: A handbook of essential theory and research*. New York: Psychology Press.

Blanch, J.M. (2012). *Trabajar y Bienestar*. Barcelona: UOC.

Blanch, J.M., Sahagún, M., Cantera, L., & Cervantes, G. (2010). Questionnaire of General Labor Wellbeing: Structure and Psychometric Properties. *Journal of Work and Organizational Psychology*, 26(2), 157–170.

Blanch, J.M., Sahagún, M., & Cervantes, G. (2010). Factor structure of Working Conditions Scale. *Journal of Work and Organizational Psychology*, 26(3), 175–189.

Cameron, K.S., & Spreitzer, G.M. (Eds.) (2011). *The Oxford Handbook of Positive Organizational Scholarship*. New York: Oxford University Press.

Choi, E., & Chentsova-Dutton, Y.E. (2016). The relationship between momentary emotions and wellbeing across European Americans, Hispanic Americans, and Asian Americans. *Cognition and emotion*, 26, 1–8.

Clark, A., & Senik, C. (Eds.) (2014). *Happiness and economic growth: Lessons from developing countries*. Oxford, UK: Oxford University Press.

Deci, E.L., & Ryan, R.M. (2008). Hedonia, eudaimonia, and wellbeing: An introduction. *Journal of Happiness Studies*, 9, 1–11.

De Neve, J.E., Diener, E., Tay, L., & Xuereb, C. (2013). The objective benefits of subjective wellbeing. In J.F. Helliwell, R. Layard, & J. Sachs (Eds.), *World happiness report 2013* (pp. 54–79). New York: UN Sustainable Development Solutions Network.

Díaz, D., Stavraki, M., Blanco, A., & Gandarillas, B. (2015). The eudaimonic component of satisfaction with life and psychological wellbeing in Spanish cultures. *Psicothema*, 27(3), 247–253.

Diener, E., Helliwell, J., & Kahneman, D. (Eds.) (2010). *International differences in wellbeing*. Oxford, UK: Oxford University Press.

Díaz, D., Blanco, A., & Durán, M. (2011). The Structure of wellbeing: The empirical encounter of three traditions. *Revista de Psicología Social*, 26, 357–372.

EU-OSHA (2013). *Wellbeing at work: creating a positive work environment*. Available at: https://osha.europa.eu/es/tools-and-publications/publications/literature_reviews/wellbeing-at-work-creating-a-positive-work-environment

EU-OSHA (2014). *Good OSH is good for business*. Available at: https://osha.europa.eu/en/tags/goodoshisgoodforbusiness

EU-OSHA (2015). *Enterprises on New and Emerging Risks (ESENER-2). Executive summary: Psychosocial risks in Europe: Prevalence and strategies for prevention*. Available at: https://osha.europa.eu/en/publications/reports/esener-ii-first-findings.pdf/view/

European Commission (2012). *Investing in wellbeing at work. Addressing psychosocial risks in times of change*. Available at: http://bookshop.europa.eu/en/investing-in-wellbeing-at-work-pbKE3110620/

EUROSTAT (2016). *Analytical report on subjective wellbeing* 2016. Available at: http://ec.europa.eu/eurostat/web/products-statistical-working-papers/-/KS-TC-16-005

Goulart, P., Blanch, J.M., Sahagún, M.A., & Bobsin, T.S. (2012). Questionário de Bem-Estar no Trabalho: Estrutura e propriedades psicométricas. *Estudos de Psicologia,* 29(1), 657–665.

Granero, A., Blanch, J.M., & Ochoa, P. (2017). Condiciones laborales y significados del trabajo de enfermería en Barcelona. *Revista Latino-Americana de Enfermagem*. In press.

Grawitch, M.J., & Ballard, D.W. (Eds.) (2016). *The Psychologically Healthy Workplace: Building a Win-Win Environment for Organizations and Employees*. Washington, DC: American Psychological Association.

Helliwell, J.F., Huang, H., & Wang, S. (2014). Social capital and wellbeing in times of crisis. *Journal of Happiness Studies*, 15(1), 145–162.

Helliwell, J.F., & Putnam, R.D. (2005). The social context of wellbeing. In F. A. Huppert, B. Keverne, & N. Baylis (Eds.), *The science of wellbeing* (pp. 435–459). London: Oxford University Press.

Huta, V., & Ryan, R.M. (2010). Pursuing pleasure or virtue: The differential and overlapping wellbeing benefits of hedonic and eudaimonic motives. *Journal of Happiness Studies*, 11, 735–762.

ILO (2012). *Decent Work Indicators. Concepts and Definitions. ILO Manual*. Geneva: ILO.

Kashdan, T.B., Biswas-Diener, R., & King, L.A. (2008). Reconsidering happiness: The costs of distinguishing between hedonics and eudaimonia. *Journal of Positive Psychology*, 3, 219–233.

Layard, R. (2011). *Happiness: lessons from a new science*. London: Penguin.

Lepeley, M.T. (2017). *Human Centered Management. The Five Pillars of Quality Organizations and Global Sustainability*. Saltaire, UK: Greenleaf.

Luthans, F., Avolio, B.J., Avey, J.B., & Norman, S.M. (2007). Positive psychological capital: Measurement and relationship with performance and satisfaction. *Personnel Psychology, 60*, 541–572.

Luthans, F., Youssef, C.M., & Avolio, B.J. (2007). *Psychological Capital. Developing the human competitive edge*. Oxford, UK: Oxford University Press.

McMahon, D. (2006). *The Pursuit of Happiness: A History from the Greeks to the present*. London: Allen Lane/Penguin.

Ochoa, P., & Blanch, J.M. (2016). Work, malaise and wellbeing in Spanish and Latin American doctors. *Revista de Saúde Pública*, 50(21), 1–14.

OECD (2013). *OECD guidelines on measuring subjective wellbeing*. Paris: OECD.

OECD (2015). *In it together: Why less inequality benefits all*. Paris: OECD.

Robertson, I., & Cooper, C. (2011). *Wellbeing. Productivity and Happiness at work*. Hampshire, UK: Palgrave-Macmillan.

Rodríguez-Carvajal, R., Moreno-Jiménez, B., de Rivas-Hermosilla, S., Álvarez-Bejarano, A., & Sanz Vergel, A.I. (2010). Positive psychology at work: Mutual gains for individuals and organizations. *Revista de Psicología del Trabajo y de las Organizaciones, 26*, 235–253.

Ryan, R.M., & Deci, E.L. (2001). To be happy or to be self-fulfilled: A review of research on hedonic and eudaimonic wellbeing. *Annual Review of Psychology, 52*, 141–166.

Ryff, C.D., & Singer, B.H. (2008). Know thyself and become what you are: A eudaimonic approach to psychological wellbeing. *Journal of Happiness Studies*, 9(1), 13–39.

Schaufeli, W.B., & Bakker, A.B. (2004). Job demands, job resources, and their relationship with burnout and engagement: A multi-sample study. *Journal of Organizational Behavior*, 25(3), 293–315.

Schulte, P., & Vainio, H. (2010). Well-being at work: Overview and perspective. *Scandinavian Journal of Work, Environment and Health*, 36(5), 422–429.

United Nations (2015). *World Happiness Report*. (Helliwell, J.F., Layard, R., & Sachs, J., Eds.). New York: UN Sustainable Development Solutions Network. Available at: http://worldhappiness.report/wp-content/uploads/sites/2/2015/04/Updated-slide-use-and-implementation.pptx

United Nations (2016). *World Happiness Report* 2016. (Helliwell, J. F., Layard, R., & Sachs, J., Eds.). New York: UN Sustainable Development Solutions Network. Available at: http://worldhappiness.report/wp-content/uploads/sites/2/2016/03/HR-V1_web.pdf

Warr, P.B. (2007). *Work, Happiness, and Unhappiness*. London: Routledge

WHO (2010). *Healthy workplaces: A WHO global model for action.* Geneva: WHO. Available at: www.who.int/occupational_health/healthy_workplaces/en/

WHO (2017). *Benefits of Workforce Health Promotion.* Available at: www.who.int/occupational_health/topics/workplace/en/index1.html

Youssef, C.M., & Luthans, F. (2010). An integrated model of Psychological Capital in the workplace. In P.A. Linley, S. Harrington, & N. Garcea (Eds.). *Oxford Handbook of Positive Psychology and Work* (pp. 277–288). Oxford, UK: Oxford University Press.

2 Wellbeing and gender parity in the workforce

Need for a new global approach

Maria-Teresa Lepeley

Do not go where the path may lead; go instead where there is no path and leave a trail.

R. W. Emerson

Introduction

Klaus Schwab, founder and executive chairman of the World Economic Forum, in the preface of the 2017 *Global Gender Gap* states that talent is an essential factor for growth and competitiveness in the world today. He calls

> to build agile economies and inclusive societies where we must ensure that women and girls are integrated as shapers and beneficiaries; otherwise global communities lose significantly in skills, ideas and new dimension critical to solve challenges and harness the opportunities we have ahead.

In January 2018, the annual Conference at the World Economic Forum emphasized gender parity in the agenda and the challenge of female empowerment as an outstanding topic, stating that giving women and girls opportunity to succeed is not only the right thing to do, but something can transform societies and economies (World Economic Forum, 2018b).

Gender parity: need for a new vision

Definitions of gender parity vary. For purposes addressed in this chapter, gender parity in the workplace refers to full awareness of the different roles women and men play in the economy and society; open access to same work opportunities and equal pay for equal responsibility; transparent salary schedules; and the value added of motherhood and its complexity in relation to the work environment.

Wellbeing in the workplace refers to optimal conditions organizations in particular and the workplace in general provide workers to maximize their engagement with work, and to develop human capital and talent to continuously improve workers' quality of life in high synchrony with organizational performance, productivity, and competitiveness goals.

Wellbeing at work and gender parity in the workplace are recurrent subjects of discussion and pressing challenges that organizations and countries worldwide face to attain sustainable growth and inclusive societies in the twenty-first century (Lepeley, 2017b). Although neither the gender gap issue nor wellbeing of women in the workplace are new items in the development agenda, they have been treated separately and the need for integration is becoming an urgent matter.

On the gender parity discussion, in spite of decades of tracking issues of discrimination against women and gender gaps, progress has been slow and old approaches have perpetuated the negative connotations that hinder solutions. Moreover, they tend to induce confrontational positions between men and women with detrimental outcomes.

I propose that organizations develop new and deliberate structures to advance gender parity planning programs in alignment with quality management strategies to build bridges between men and women instead of continuing to dwell on gender gaps (Lepeley, 2017a). After discussing arguments for gender parity in the workplace that require special attention, at the end of the chapter I present the reasons that justify the need for a common ground and approaches to improve wellbeing for all as a necessary condition for success and workplace improvement.

Different roles, shared gains

Historically, the workplace has been the intrinsic place for men, as workers and bread winners – as the house has been for women, as child-bearers and care-givers. Men have traditionally worked outside the house to earn an income. Women have been responsible for the domestic manufacturing of products and services without monetary compensation. But things have changed. The participation of women in the workforce started to increase at a faster pace late in the last three decades of the twentieth century and it accelerated in the twenty-first century.

I don't think that gender disparity is a problem of inequality. To a large extent it is the result of historical events and cultural developments that were not planned with deliberate purpose to cause harm to women. The roots of gender disparity are embedded in human nature, in genomic, genetic, and psychosocial differences between men and women that have perpetuated and not changed as fast as the world is changing. Gender disparity is a problem of omission, misconception, and miscommunication. I say this based on the personal experience I will relate next, and after observing gender trends in changing times and relationships between men and women in different generations and societies in different countries.

Nevertheless I do acknowledge claims of women who suffer sexual harassment in the workplace, across industries and around the world. This is a most disturbing problem for women and society that it is often dominating the news (Denning, 2017). Sexual harassment is a complex dilemma that needs close attention. I show statistics in next sections. But in this chapter I concentrate on global comparisons of gender parity and women's economic and social roles that impact the workplace and have received low attention until now. As a woman, I expect that the new vision I propose to solve these old gender gaps and new obstacles to wellbeing in the workplace would lead to solutions. New approaches must have high awareness that gender parity and human wellbeing are a road, not a destiny. They are ongoing processes in constant adjustment and continuous need for analysis and improvement.

O'Brien *et al.* (2017) state that, despite decades of research and intervention, workplace gender disparity remains a worldwide issue because women are under-represented in leadership roles, over-represented in unpaid labor, and earn less than men for same work. The study conveys that gender disparities in the workplace are a "wicked problem," resulting from interactions between multiple factors that are a symptom and a cause of other problems; it is surrounded by a significant amount of disagreement and ambiguity about what needs to be done to reach gender parity.

Institutions like the International Labor Organization ILO, Gallup Organization, the World Economic Forum WEF, the World Bank, United Nations, and the International Monetary Fund, among many others, despite their tendency to refer to the gender gap and discrimination in the literature, in reality all are confronting acute challenges and promoting the need to increase gender parity. The problem is that most organizations are considering gender parity in isolation from well-being in the workplace and this segmented approach significantly increases obstacles to finding solutions.

Women's view complements and expands men's vision, and vice versa

The following experience I describe helped me understand gender parity from a different and positive perspective, in contrast with negative gender gaps expressions I had often heard.

Early in the 1980s after I finished a graduate degree in education, I transferred to graduate studies in economics. I was the first student at the University of Miami to make such a drastic disciplinary change. The change was not only profound in terms of discipline but in other dimensions as well. While in education women were the majority, in the Department of Economics, located in the School of Business, only 10 percent of the students were women. All the professors were men. I was new in a very different environment and had much to learn and deal within a new, very different discipline that required significant mental and behavioral adjustments. I recall that in class when I asked questions of professors (who were unaware that I had transferred from education) they looked at me somewhat surprised, and a few with a certain disdain. My questions were certainly different, and some were not easy for them to answer. Time went by. At graduation, some instructors and numerous male classmates were sincere enough to tell me: "Maria-Teresa, because of your unusual questions in class I learned to see economics from different and broader dimensions." I highly valued their honesty because they had also taught me an important lesson: men may see things differently, but earnest and open discussions lead to better understanding and building bridges. Those men did not intend to harm me with their ironic smiles or glances of contempt. But they had never stood in the place of a woman or seen economics the way I did.

Fathers make a difference for their daughters and gender parity

I realize that sometimes women prefer to avoid the inconvenience of interacting with men who make statement they dislike, due to shyness or the desire to avoid confrontation. In this respect I was different from women of my generation. I was fortunate to have a father who encouraged me to inquire, discuss, and debate respectfully. He taught me that, as a woman, in an age and cultural context where men prevailed, I could reach out and debate if I was courteous and clever, and respected opinions of other people. I share this personal story because it conveys how gender parity can create bridges between women and men instead of deepening gender gaps. New articles support the effect of fathers on assertive daughters (Denning, 2017).

Gender parity challenges in economics

My experience happened three decades ago. But things have not changed much. A recent article about the participation of women in economics reveals low improvement (Gittleson, 2017). A second-year student of economics at a university in the UK noticed that her male and female classmates approached economic problems differently, leading to more comprehensive analysis. She then decided to make every effort to increase the number of women studying economics.

The argument here is that, while the emphasis at the moment in education is to open access and attract more women to STEM fields (science, technology, engineering, and math), few realize the urgency for more women to study economics in order to understand and advise about important economic implications for women in the workforce and society.

In 2017, in the US only 13 percent of academic tenured positions in economics were held by women; in the UK this is 15.5 percent. Only one woman has received the Nobel Prize in economics – American Elinor Ostrom in 2009 – since the award was established in 1968. In Germany, the Council of Economic Experts, a top group of advisors to the government, has one woman among its five members, offering a 20 percent representation. She has been part of the Council since 2014 and was the last member to join CEE[1].

For those of us who believe in free choice, these figures may not demonstrate gender bias per se, but personal preferences. Of course, we cannot force women to study economics. It was hard for me and not all women want to make a similar effort. Women can be thinking rationally when they avoid economics and choose other disciplines better suited for their interests and skills.

But there are some key questions related to economics in particular, as it is an essential science in the promotion of holistic human progress. Why do so few women study economics? What needs to be done to encourage more women to study economics? Is the economic profession doing enough to attract women? This line of inquiry is important because today economics looks at world problems through the eyes of men only, therefore covering only half of the human story. This implies that most economic decisions are made with a partial vision. The results I show next support these concerns.

Building gender parity in the world starts building bridges in the workplace

The World Economic Forum (WEF) promotes gender parity as a critical driver of GDP growth in countries around the world. WEF estimates that the attainment of gender parity would allow the UK to increase GDP by US \$250 billion, the US by US \$1.750 billion, Japan by US \$550 billion, France by US \$320 billion, Germany by US \$320 billion, and China US \$2.5 trillion. Globally GDP could increase US \$5.3 trillion by 2025 by increasing economic participation of women by 25 percent (World Economic Forum, 2017). WEF estimates that, at the current pace of efforts, if there is no deterioration, global gender parity could be achieved in about 100 years. The most stubborn limitations for gender parity are in the economic and political dimensions. If progress does not accelerate, reaching economic parity would take 217 years. This is one of many reasons why it is so important that more women study economics and participate actively in development policies.

Now it is critical to note that GDP is a monetary accounting objective method to measure economic growth. But GDP excludes the consideration of subjective wellbeing that people accrue from intangible benefits. A sizable portion of the subjective contribution is generated by women in unpaid production of products and service. Women use their human capital and talent to provide better care to their children and families, making significant contributions to the common good and society. None of these benefits are accounted for in the GDP formula (Lepeley, 2017b).

To solve GDP shortcomings, new development indexes are appearing that are centered on happiness, such as the World Happiness Report (Helliwell *et al.*, 2017), supported by the United Nations. In a study I conducted on Bhutan, the country that developed and was the first to implement the Gross National Happiness (GNH) Index in 1971 to measure *happiness* of the population as a keynote for progress, I found that GNH and GDP are indeed complements not substitutes. I argue for the need to integrate them to measure real progress leading to sustainable development (Lepeley, 2017b). This is basically because, after family and social affiliations, the most pressing need for people in Bhutan is to have an income. Money does not buy happiness, in Bhutan or anywhere; but income is a necessary condition for quality of life for men and women to attain long-term sustainable wellbeing, beyond temporary feelings of happiness.

Remaining disparities

Income and wage disparity is a global problem that inhibits the participation of women in labor markets. Although recent studies conducted by the International Labor Organization (ILO) and the Gallup Organization (2017) report that the majority of women prefer to work in paid jobs, many are discouraged due to wage differences.

Globally the wage disparity reveals that women earn 23 percent less than men. Gallup and ILO (2017) report that this differential is not related to the level of economic development of a country, because countries with a high level of income per capita also show larger wage disparities. Wage disparities can neither be explained by differences in education between men and women, nor by experience, age, or career breaks. ILO attributes wage differences "to pervasive discrimination – conscious or unconscious – against women." Furthermore ILO-Gallup states that working mothers suffer additional wage penalties, and generally earn less than working women without dependent children and significantly less than fathers with similar employment and household responsibilities.

A view of gender parity around the world

To have an idea of where we need to go we need clarity where we are today. Table 2.1 shows levels of gender parity by world regions. A substantial broad variance is clear between Western European countries, which show the highest level of gender parity, and the Middle East / North Africa with the lowest.

As expected, developed countries have higher level of gender parity than developing nations. On the positive side this means that developing countries have potential to accrue higher benefits increasing efforts to attain gender parity at a faster pace than they have done until now.

In terms of the structure of gender parity the Gallup-ILO study (2017) distinguishes four dimensions: health and survival, educational attainment, economic participation and opportunity, and political empowerment. World results are shown in Table 2.2.

Table 2.1 Gender parity by region.

Rank	Region	% Gender Parity
1	Western Europe	75
2	North America (USA & Canada)	72
3	Eastern Europe & Central Asia	71
4	Latin America & the Caribbean	70
5	East Asia / Pacific	68
6	GLOBAL AVERAGE	68
7	South Sahara / Africa	68
8	South Asia	68
9	Middle East / North Africa	60

Source: 2017 Global Gender Gap, World Economic Forum.

Table 2.2 Dimensions of gender parity.

Rank	Dimension	% parity	Assessment variables (ratio men/women)
1	Health & survival	96	Birth ratio, life expectancy
2	Education attainment	95	Literacy rate, primary enrolment, secondary enrolment, tertiary enrolment
3	Economic participation and opportunity	58	Labor participation, wage equity, earn income, wealth, legislators, senior officials, professional and technical workers
4	Political empowerment	23	Seats in parliament, positions in ministerial level, number of years with female head of state

Source: Gallup and ILO report, 2017.

Although most countries have attained relatively high levels of gender parity in health and education, 96 percent and 95 percent respectively, remaining disparities are significant in the economic participation of women (58 percent) and particularly in political empowerment (23 percent).

The ongoing discussion on low gender parity in economic participation and political empowerment may demonstrate, again, that women are making rational decisions. This assumption supports the hypothesis that instead of maximizing economic gains in paid jobs, women find higher subjective benefits devoting more time to care for their children and families.

In the political arena, growing disappointment with the political class is hindering women's participation worldwide.

On the practical side, these results have deep implications and show the high costs of failures in society. Particularly due to dislocation in education and mis-allocations in educational systems anchored to obsolete models that neglect to provide adequate education for women in disciplines with deep gender disparities, such as STEM, economics, and political sciences, among others. Stubborn educational problems also affect boys and men, curtailing their life potential.

In spite of almost universal access to education for girls and women around the world, education is far from complying with its most critical responsibilities: preparing girls and women to meet the challenges of labor markets and political participation.

Women's preferences and employment

Table 2.3 shows the sectors where women are working worldwide. It is remarkable to observe the shortcomings of education. For over a century women are concentrated in health, education, public administration and the non-profit sector. This is important data that requires further analysis to uncover future implications of gender parity.

Table 2.3 Talent pool: female share of employment preferences.

Rank	Sector	% participation
1.	Health care	61
2.	Education	59
3.	Non profit	57
4.	Legal	50
5.	Public administration	50
6.	Media / communication	50
7.	Corporate services	46
8.	Real estate	45
9.	Finance	41
10.	Information technology	27
11.	Energy / mining / engineering	25
12.	Manufacturing	23

Source: 2017 Global Gender Gap, World Economic Forum.

Disparities in workforce participation

Although women represent more than half of the working age population (15 and older) only 50 percent participate in the labor market, compared with 76 percent of men. Compared with the global standard the participation of women is low. Table 2.4 shows workforce participation by gender and region. The region that shows the highest participation of women in the labor market is South Sahara (65 percent), followed by Eastern Asia (62 percent). The gap between the participation of men and women is larger in Arab States (76 percent to 21 percent respectively), Northern Africa (74 percent to 23 percent), and South Eastern Asia and the Pacific (79 percent to 28 percent). While North, South and West Europe (64 percent to 51 percent) and North America (68 percent to 56 percent) show the highest levels of gender parity in this global ranking.

Table 2.4 Workforce participation by gender and region.

Region	Men %	Women %
North, Southern, Western Europe	64	51
Eastern Europe	68	53
North America	68	56
Latin America & the Caribbean	78	53
Eastern Asia	77	21
Central & Western Asia	73	44
South Eastern Asia & the Pacific	79	28
Northern Africa	74	23
South Sahara Africa	76	65
Arab States	76	21

Source: Gallup and ILO report, 2017.

Gender parity and women in the workplace

The global study conducted by ILO and Gallup (2017) titled *Towards a Better Future for Women at Work. Voices from Women and Men* about needs men and women related to work preferences concludes that the majority of women prefer to work a paid job and men largely agree. The report states that, although gender parity has not been achieved, the general perception is that the attitudes of men and women are closer now than ever before in regards to women and paid work. Overall the most important challenge men and women agree about working women is the need to balance work and family responsibilities. Although this is the most critical challenge working women face, there are others.

Women in developed countries most often cite unequal pay for similar work. And women in developing countries mention unfair treatment and abuse in the workplace among the most important challenges.

Work preferences among women also vary with age. Table 2.5 shows that women in the 15–29 age group prefer a combination of a paid job and time to stay at home, commonly to take care of their children. This preference is similar among women in the 30–44 age cohort for the same reason. Women in the 45–64 and 65+ age cohorts show a preference for staying at home instead of working for pay. Studies conducted by Kuschel and Lepeley (2017, 2016) and Lepeley *et al.* (2015) show that women in these age groups do not stay at home or remain inactive, but they realize they have accrued substantial amount of knowledge and experience and prefer to have freedom to start a business project of their own. This option provides them with more flexibility to combine work and family responsibilities than strict job schedules in paid work in organizations that enforce restrictive labor laws and policies that obstruct work flexibility.

Table 2.6 shows that the type of challenges that women face in the workplace also vary by age cohort. Globally women in the 15–29 age cohort cite unfair treatment and harassment at work as main constraints. Women in the 30–44 age group mention lack of affordable care for children and family as the main challenge. Women in older groups highlight unequal pay as the main constraint.

Table 2.7 shows that for most women work–family balance and affordable child care are the most pressing challenges. Therefore these are the problem areas that require most attention and fast solutions in the workplace.

Women also perceive unfair treatment as an important constraint in paid work as shown in Table 2.7. Unfair treatment is more difficult to identify and solve

Table 2.5 % women's preference to work for paid job, stay at home, or both.

Age group	Work pay job	Both	Stay home	Don't know
15–29	28	39	29	4
30–44	20	38	38	4
45–64	20	32	44	4
65+	18	30	42	9

Source: Gallup and ILO report, 2017.

Table 2.6 Main constraints by women's age cohorts in paid work.

Age group	Main constraints
15–28	Unfair treatment; harassment at work
30–44	Lack of affordable care for children and family members
Older women	Unequal pay

Source: Gallup and ILO report, 2017.

Table 2.7 Main constraints women with paid jobs mention (global).

Rank	Constraint
1.	Work–family balance
2.	Affordable child care
3.	Unfair treatment
4.	Lack of flexible hours
5.	Lack of good paid job
6.	Unequal pay
7.	Disapproval of women working
8.	Safe transportation

Source: Gallup and ILO report, 2017.

because it covers a large number of dimensions and degrees that affect not only women but to a large extent also men in the labor force.

ILO programs and policies to increase gender parity and improve general wellbeing in the workforce

Table 2.8 shows the seven areas where ILO calls for special attention to be paid to increase the wellbeing of all workers in the workforce with a special focus on advancing gender parity. Efforts to attain these objectives and the programs and policies deployed require deep changes in working conditions and organizational cultures across the workplace to increase the potential of positive income (Javed, 2017). Increasingly organizations in all sectors in countries around the world are adopting human-centered management models to transform old process focused organizational structures of the industrial past that no longer work in the Knowledge Economy (Lepeley, 2017a).

Women in leadership

Women in leadership is a critical dimension of gender parity. But until now it has been a complex problem because there is no clear understanding of the implications that affect women, not inside but outside the workforce, and what needs to be done to promote change with effective policies. In spite of the efforts of companies

Table 2.8 ILO policies to improve gender parity.

Rank	Area of attention	Critical points
1.	Decent work	Opportunity to access productive work for men and women that secures freedom, equity, dignity, and fair income.
2.	Family supportive policies	Improve access of women to labor markets to promote economic empowerment and increase gender parity.
		ILO 1981 Workers With Family Responsibilities Convention to provide "effective equality of opportunity and treatment between men and women workers with family responsibilities."[2]
3.	Policies to increase gender parity	Early marriage, pregnancy and unpaid child care are persistent barriers for women to enter education and the labor force.
		Need for programs and policies aimed to facilitate school-to-work transition.
		Macroeconomic policies to open women equal access to employment.
		Labor policies that promote maternity protection and leave provisions offering flexible schedules, and optimal child and eldercare, through employer or the state.
4.	Maternity protection	Safe maternity and mother's health are central elements of decent and productive work for women.
		Maternity protection needs to ensure wellbeing of mother and newborn child, to unable women successfully combine reproductive and productive roles, prevent unequal treatment due to women's reproductive role.
		ILO has Maternity Protection Convention (2000).[3]
		Although ILO has no convention on fathers' role, it recognizes that paternity leaves offer fathers an important opportunity to bond with their newborn child and allow them to get more involved with family responsibilities at home. ILO recognizes that fathers' involvement in early childcare has positive effects on children's development and health.
		ILO acknowledges that increased participation of men in household activities helps women, allowing them to achieve better work–family balance.
5.	Affordable care and flexible work	Affordable care for children but also for the elderly are variables that affect work–family wellbeing. As the world population grows and ages, so does the demand for quality care and women's responsibilities.
		Childcare and eldercare was identified as barrier number one for women's leadership.
6.	Gender parity compensation and wages	173 countries have ratified (1951) ILO's Equal Remuneration Convention, in which the central issue is "the value of job performed" instead of "equal pay for equal work." This means that men and women work in different jobs, and comparing jobs alone does not address the full range of discrimination issues in paid work.
7.	Violence and harassment at work	A tripartite discussion of the ILO with the International Labour Conference and the International Parliament of Labour is scheduled for June 2018 to discuss "violence and harassment against women and men in the workplace."
		Sexual harassment that disproportionally affects women at work diminishes quality of working life and jeopardizes wellbeing, with cost implications for organizations.

Source: Gallup and ILO report, 2017.

to increase the participation of women in leadership – opening access to executive positions, and offering incentive packages and fringe benefits to promote women – until now efforts worldwide have not produced the expected results.

Role models are useful and necessary to stimulate women in leadership. But results of longitudinal programs designed and supported by organizations, sectors, national laws, and international agreements and conventions show limited progress. In the business sectors, where there are special interests in promoting women to leadership positions in order to expand market share and attract a broader client base, results are slim. Even in countries with the best records of women in leadership positions, representation is below a third.

A global study on diversity conducted in 2018 by the McKinsey company shows evidence of the limited participation of women in leadership in the business sector. The study confirms that the relationship between gender and financial performance in companies holds across geographical boundaries, with some variation in different regions. The cross-country study of women in leadership shows three countries at the top. All of them have the most advanced market economies in the world. Table 2.9 shows the three countries with highest percentage of women in leadership: Australia, the United States and the United Kingdom. Australia has the highest participation of women in leadership in business companies as shown by women's participation in Executive Boards and Boards of Directors (21 percent and 30 percent respectively).

Part of the low participation of women in leadership positions is due to biased organizational environments and cultures, and persistent traditions across countries and around the world (Hunt *et al.*, 2018). But from my point of view, as a woman and an economist, these results also signal women's choice and preferences. Women assign more value to family duties and a high reluctance to trade leadership advantages for the long-term benefits associated with family responsibilities, and overall with successful motherhood and supporting their children from crib to independency. Mothers realize that all their investments in time and care raising their children to attain the highest possible standards in life, work and society have significantly higher returns than any other investment they make in life. Fathers are increasingly aware of these returns and are increasingly participating and sharing household duties and parenthood (Kuschel & Lepeley, 2016).

From the workplace dimension, studies confirm that, when organizations display gender parity in structures and strategies, women's leadership positively impacts

Table 2.9 Female leadership in business.

Country	Average % women working in companies	% women in Executive Boards in the country	% women in Boards of Directors in the country
Australia	40	21	30
United States	34	19	28
United Kingdom	32	15	22

Source: Hunt *et al.*, 2018.

performance and productivity. In contrast, when gender parity conditions do not exist or are poorly implemented participation of women in leadership is neglected affecting performance negatively (Murray & Southey, 2017).

Global policies to improve gender parity in the workforce

The World Economic Forum is presenting gender parity as one of the most important points on the agenda at the annual 2018 Conference in Davos (World Economic Forum 2018a, 2018b, 2018c). Discussions include a concrete proposal of five recommendations that management teams and organizations worldwide need to observe and act upon decisively to improve gender quality. A summary is presented in Table 2.10.

A prominent wellbeing challenge in the workplace with regrettable gender parity

Up to now I have primarily discussed situations that affect women in the workplace and the need for new approaches to increase gender parity. I have emphasized that solutions will have to build bridges between women and men in the workplace, the economy, and society at large to decrease the gender gaps that prevail. But this book and this chapter are anchored on the analysis of the wellbeing of all

Table 2.10 WEF 2018 five gender parity recommendations.

Recommendation	Implementation
Make gender parity a strategic objective for the organization	Deploy gender parity as the top-down commitment imperative. Gender parity strengthens organizational culture of accountability, quality and parity.
Eliminate gender stereotypes linked to work-life balance programs	Change organizational culture promoting gender-neutral flexible career paths. Actively encourage all employees to take advantage of these opportunities.
Modify performance review process	Eliminate structural disadvantages for people who seize work–life balance opportunities. Do not penalize employees for additional work flexibility.
Systematize data collection to continuously assess progress	Gender parity metrics facilitate dialogue and conversations based on facts, rather than speculation. Establish common ground for open and honest gender parity discussions in workplace.
Gender balance recruitment strategies	Avoid rigid quotas. Search for a balanced talent pool at all levels of the organization.

Source: 2018 Annual Conference, World Economic Forum.

people in the workplace. So I end this gender parity discussion calling for special attention to an unbiased, yet stubborn and massive wellbeing problem that pervades the workplace worldwide: less than a third of all workers in full-time paid employment around the world feel engaged and happy with the level of wellbeing in the work they do on a daily basis. But over two-thirds of all workers report they are struggling or suffering with working conditions.

There are increasing volumes of evidence that wellbeing at work is essential for workers to maximize engagement and performance and for organizations to optimize productivity and competitiveness (Lepeley, 2017a). Gallup's results from a worldwide survey reveal outstanding levels of misuse, waste of human capital, and squandering of talent that is weakening the workforce. Unless effective programs and policies are aimed at improving the wellbeing of all men and women in the workplace, hardly any of the gender parity challenges in the workplace identified above will succeed.

The global study conducted by Gallup in 142 countries illustrates a troubling picture. And here, in the four dimensions considered, there is gender parity, for good or bad, between men and women. And women show somewhat better results than men.

Table 2.11 shows that, worldwide, less than a third of full-time workers, 25 percent of men and 29 percent of women, feel they are thriving, engaged with their daily work, and satisfied with their job and the level of wellbeing. The majority of people feel they are struggling with conditions at work (61 percent of men and 60 percent of women), and a considerable proportion reports they are suffering with the work they perform on a daily basis (13 percent of men and 11 percent of women) as shown in Table 2.11.

From the human perspective, these results show the difficult and dreadful conditions most workers face in the workforce, and also when they are unemployed (searching and not finding) or out of work (not searching).

From the organizational dimension this is the heaviest burden on productivity and competitiveness that will increasingly challenge sustainability. That's why wellbeing at work needs to be the matter of highest concern for management and organizations. The high proportion of people in full-time employment who feel disengaged and dissatisfied with working conditions is a high concern for economists and governments worldwide who are responsible for optimizing productivity and economic growth to build inclusive societies.

Table 2.11 % global life evaluation by employment status.

	Global Total		Full-time Employment		Unemployed		Out of work	
	Men	*Women*	*Men*	*Women*	*Men*	*Women*	*Men*	*Woman*
Thriving	22	24	25	29	14	19	21	22
Struggling	64	61	62	60	70	68	64	61
Suffering	14	15	13	11	16	13	15	17

Source: Gallup and ILO report, 2017.

Conclusions

In contrast with past experiences, today increasing numbers of international development organizations, scholars, women and men worldwide have consensus about the urgency to increase gender parity as a critical element of social stability and an economic development priority. Most are aware of the high costs of postponing solutions at national and global scales if the world continues deploying sluggish and obsolete strategies of the past. But most are unaware that gender parity is one element of the larger workforce challenge: human wellbeing for all.

To advance gender parity within the context of wellbeing in the workplace requires that organizations in all sectors, nations and worldwide understand the high value women in the workforce assign first and foremost to raising their children. Women, and increasingly men, are aware that the success of their children in life provides the highest returns to any investment they can do, monetary and non-monetary. To be effective, gender parity programs and policies must account for the multi-jobs mothers have aside from their paid jobs. Overall promotion of women's participation in the workforce needs perfect synchronization between value-added motherhood and fathers' participation as imperatives in the design of social and economic policies to advance gender parity with integral wellbeing in the workplace.

Furthermore, the same obstacles that affect mothers in the workplace, are affecting increasing numbers of young women in childbearing age who postpone marriage, avoid committed partnerships or motherhood and now are realizing the costs of their decisions versus the benefits of a family.

Although the record of global gender parity in the workplace has improved in the twenty-first century, the sources consulted estimate that if the world advances at the same pace it would take a century to attain gender parity. But the argument I post here is that a) the gender parity challenges are irrevocably embedded in the greater challenge of wellbeing for all in the workplace, and b) given the state of the world in terms of facilitating technology, abundant knowledge and shared interests of men and women, reaching gender parity and wellbeing improvement could be accelerate.

New initiative need to increase awareness about tangible and overall intangible benefits that men, families , communities, the workforce, the economy and inclusive societies, derive from women in paid jobs and unpaid work. Plus *urbi et orbe* information about the surmounting costs associated with postponing progress of wellbeing in the workplace that are a significant obstruction for gender parity.

Organizations that neglect workers' wellbeing and underestimate the benefit of gender parity are avoiding their main duties: continuous performance improvement, productivity, and competitiveness required to attain sustainability in the twenty-first century (Lepeley, 2015, 2017a, 2017b). All labor programs and policies aimed to advance gender parity in the workplace will fail unless there is optimal synchrony between people's wellbeing and GDP growth to secure sustainability and inclusive societies founded on shared responsibility of men and women.

Acknowledgment

This chapter is the result of conversations with Paola Ochoa, the principal editor of this book – comparing women's experiences. While I am a proud grandmother of 5, from a son and a daughter, Paola is expecting her first daughter, Victoria Alegría. My advice: to invest in our children has the highest return a mother can expect in life, but also fathers and society at large. I am grateful to Roland Bardy, Associate Editor of our Routledge Human Centered Management Book Series, and to Ronald Tarr, José Manuel Saiz-Alvarez, and Peter Essens for their valuable feedback.

Notes

1. German Council of Economic Experts: www.sachverstaendigenrat-wirtschaft.de/ratsmitglieder.html?&L=1
2. This Convention calls for compliance with following norms: prohibiting discrimination in employment against workers with family responsibilities; supporting employment allowing work–family balance; family-friendly working time arrangements, provision of family friendly facilities such as childcare; provision of training to help workers with family responsibilities to become and remain integrated into the workforce and to re-enter the workforce after an absence due to these responsibilities (Gallup & ILO, 2017).
3. This Convention includes: maternity leave for 14 weeks around the birth of the child; health protection in the workplace for pregnant and breastfeeding women; cash for medical needs; employment protection and non-discrimination.

References

Denning, S. (2017). Is Gender Parity Even Possible? *Forbes*. Accessed January 2018. www.forbes.com/sites/stephaniedenning/2017/11/13/is-gender-parity-even-possible/

Gallup & International Labor Organization. (2017). Toward a Better Future for Women at Work. Voices of Women and Men. http://news.gallup.com/reports/204785/ilo-gallup-report-towards-better-future-women-work-voices-women-men.aspx

Gittleson, K. (2017). Where Are All the Women in Economics? *BBC Business*. October 13. Accessed January 2018. www.bbc.com/news/business-41571333

Helliwell, J., Layard, R., & Sachs, J. (2017). World Happiness Report. http://world happiness.report/ed/2017/

Hunt, V., Price, S., Dixon-Fyle, S., & Yee, L. (2018). Delivering Through Diversity. *McKinsey*. Accessed January 2018. www.mckinsey.com/business-functions/organization/our-insights/delivering-through-diversity

Javed, U. (2017). Work/Family Conflict and Employee Wellbeing: The Buffering Effects of Workplace Resources. *Academy of Management Procedures*, *2017*, 11080.

Kuschel, K., & Lepeley, M.T. (2016). Copreneurial Women in Start-ups: Growth-oriented or Lifestyle? An Aid for Technology Industry Investors. *Academia Revista Latinoamericana de Administración, 29*(2), 1–19.

Kuschel, K., Lepeley, M.T., Espinosa, F., & Gutiérrez, S. (2017). Funding Challenges of Latin American Women Startup Founders in the Technology Industry. *Cross Cultural & Strategic Management, 24*(2), 310–331.

Lepeley, M.T. (2017a). *Human Centered Management: The Five Global Pillars of Organization Quality and Sustainability.* Saltaire, UK: Greenleaf.

Lepeley, M.T. (2017b). Bhutan's Gross National Happiness: An Approach to Human Centred Sustainable Development. *South Asian Journal of Human Resource Management*, *4*(2), 174–184.

Lepeley, M.T., Pizarro, O., & Mandakovic, V. (2015). Women Entrepreneurs in Chile: Three Decades of Challenges and Lessons in Innovation and Business Sustainability. In V. Ramadani, S. Gërguri-Rashiti, & A. Fayolle. (Eds.), *Female Entrepreneurship in Transition Economies Trends and Challenges*. Palgrave Macmillan.

Murray, P., & Southey, K. (2017). Minimising the Gender Status Effects on Performance of Women in Leadership. *Academy of Management Procedures*, *2017*, 14500.

O'Brien, K, William Fitzsimmons, T., Crane, M. Head, B. (2017). Workplace gender inequality as a Wicked Problem: Implications for research and practice. *Academy of Management Procedures*, *2017*, 14717.

World Economic Forum. (2017). 2017 Global Gender Gap. www.weforum.org/reports/the-global-gender-gap-report-2017

World Economic Forum. (2018a). Annual Conference Davos: 5 things that must change to end gender inequality at work. Accessed January 2018. www.weforum.org/agenda/2017/02/5-things-that-must-change-to-end-gender-inequality-at-work

World Economic Forum. (2018b). Annual Conference Davos: Why 2018 must be the year for women to thrive. Accessed January 2018. www.weforum.org/agenda/2018/01/the-time-has-come-for-women-to-thrive-heres-how/

World Economic Forum. (2018c). Annual Conference Davos: Will the Fourth Industrial Revolution be a revolution for women? www.weforum.org/agenda/2018/01/gender-inequality-and-the-fourth-industrial-revolution.

3 Wellbeing in organizations

Dimensions and intersections

Nicky R.M. Pouw

Introduction

In economics in general, and business economics' organizational and management studies in particular, there is a growing trend to pay more attention to issues of social inclusion to advance corporate sustainability (Bardy & Massaro, 2012; Likoko & Janvier 2017; Kourula *et al.*, 2017). I argue that economics would benefit from focusing more on human wellbeing and how people and organizations strive to improve economic wellbeing rather than focusing exclusively on money (Pouw & McGregor, 2014; McGregor & Pouw, 2016; Pouw 2017), in order to gain relevance in the economic policymaking and practices that converge with daily lives of people, which is the ultimate mission of all social sciences. Therefore the same applies to business economics, and organization and management studies, when much attention is placed on system thinking and the control of technical, managerial, and financial factors that influence measurable performance while the human being remains strikingly invisible – or a narrow stereotype of a rational actor that can be controlled like any other input of production.

As a result, human wellbeing as a component of organizational sustainability is overlooked. One exception is Elinor Ostrom's work on public choice and poly-centricity of governance system (Ostrom & Williamson, 2000; Ostrom, 2010), which is built on Schumpeter's organizational theory.

In this chapter, I conceptually and analytically elaborate the notion that human wellbeing evolves from convergence of internal and external strategies of organizational sustainability. The chapter is organized as follows. In the second section, the concept of human wellbeing is defined and explained beyond the assumption of individual welfare. In the third section, human wellbeing is operationalized from three dimensions: material, relational and subjective wellbeing, different dimensions that intersect in complex trade-offs. Human striving for continuous wellbeing improvement is discussed in the fourth section. In the fifth section, the relevance of human wellbeing in relation to organizational sustainability is explored, a strategic focus on economic wellbeing is proposed, and a distinction is made between internal and external strategies for organizational sustainability. The sixth section concludes by exploring new directions.

Defining human wellbeing

What is "human wellbeing"? Allister McGregor, in his pioneering research on human wellbeing and development in low income countries, defines human wellbeing as a state of being satisfied in relation to others, where human needs are met, and where people are free to pursue meaningful life goals to achieve satisfactory quality of life (McGregor, 2007). This definition of wellbeing assumes that human beings are social beings and that every human being stands and develops in relation with other people.

This social relationship is not always based on a voluntary choice. In families, organizations, neighborhoods, and many other social groupings people are interconnected *prima facie*. In addition, every human being is also living in relation to time and a certain spirit of time that includes a past, present and future.

Awareness of these implications helps to understand that people make economic decisions in relation to other human beings, their life environment, and emotions besides self-interest. People think and act, either consciously or unconsciously, in relation to other people around them in their daily life and working environment.

Besides, people make economic decisions with a long-term view. People think ahead, back and forth, and make complex decisions about time. This means that human wellbeing is a highly dynamic concept.

Wellbeing is both an outcome and a process of human pursuit for protection, stability, and improvement. The concept of wellbeing includes comprehensive understanding of the relational aspects of the human being. In addition, wellbeing has objective and subjective dimensions. Thus, every person has an objective need for food and drink, a sense of security and freedom, but the extent to which and in which form is subjective.

Human wellbeing, as a process and an outcome, is subjective because not every person pursues the same life goals, or acts based on the same conviction. Material wealth does not guarantee relational stability or happiness or life satisfaction. Material, relational, and subjective wellbeing are interrelated. Advances in one dimension can also undermine, stabilize, or reinforce advances in other dimensions.

Human wellbeing means something different and beyond welfare. Welfare, in the history of economic science, is commonly equated with the individual pursuit of a better life. However, it is debatable if original thinkers on welfare really had such a narrow concept of welfare in mind. Adam Smith's "Theory of Moral Sentiments" from 1759, for example, shows that he considered nature as one of the greatest sources of human prosperity. Over time, the field of economics that is understood as the pursuit of the individual maximization of welfare has become synonymous with the maximization of social welfare. But in reality maximizing individual welfare may come at a cost for nature and of social welfare. It doesn't simply add up. Social welfare takes into account relative issues of common welfare such as inequality, and in what ways and *under what* conditions individual welfare is pursued in relation to others in society and the environment. This forces the consideration of the quality and sustainability of production, consumption, and distribution processes in the economy.

The above assumption of "methodological individualism" has been debated for decades by heterodox economists as well as by multiple disciplines outside economics. The critics argue that any escalation of individual welfare to a higher economic level, for example from individual to household, firm or national level, is accompanied by an exchange of other values that influence and transform the ultimate welfare outcome achieved. In other words, a qualitative transformation of the welfare relationship between people or organizations takes place, implying that aggregate welfare can be greater or smaller than the sum of individual parts by effects of complement or substitution.

Implicit in an alternative approach is a broader concept of welfare – where more than income or other one-dimensional material values are taken into account, and for which Allister McGregor and I propose the concept of human wellbeing is enchanced (McGregor & Pouw, 2016).

Wellbeing refers to "a state of being in relation to others." It is then in this relationship that it can work in a positive or negative way, thus strengthening or attenuating the relationship. Wellbeing is more than living well as an individual; it means *living well together* (Deneulin & McGregor, 2010; McGregor, 2011).

Dimensions of human wellbeing

Human wellbeing is thus far more comprehensive than welfare. Human wellbeing requires identification to facilitate application. McGregor (2007) makes an analytical distinction between three dimensions of wellbeing:

(i)   Material wellbeing: objectively perceptible outcomes that people achieve, such as nutrition, housing, property, income, work.
(ii) Relational wellbeing: people have relationships with others that enable to fulfil personal needs and goals, including civil rights and responsibilities, security, self-determination, power, partnerships, networks.
(iii) Subjective wellbeing: meanings and values people assign to needs and goals they can achieve and process in contentment, frustration, conflict, uncertainty, happiness.

These three dimensions of human wellbeing are closely linked. Besides, all aspects of material and relational wellbeing are subject to subjective evaluation. The differences among the three dimensions of wellbeing are purely analytical, but in practice sometimes difficult to recognize. For example, is "health" a material aspect of wellbeing, relational or subjective? I analyze the three dimensions of human wellbeing to demonstrate differences with economic wellbeing in organizations, which are addressed in the fourth section.

By and large, the economic behavior of people is characterized by a constant endeavor to protect, maintain, or improve economic wellbeing (e.g. increasing income, assets, labor conditions, job satisfaction); as individual, group, organization or society.

The extent of people's economic wellbeing depends on resources, competences, relations, and the freedom they have at their disposal. Sometimes, within a group or an organization, a person can access more resources or higher capacity, or gain more freedoms to attain life goals. Therefore, joining a community group, professional association, or a political party may be a key strategy for some people to enhance their power and voice.

Continuous wellbeing improvement

However, it would be simplistic to assume that "human wellbeing" is a matter of choice; because not every human being has the power or means to make reasonable choices, let alone make such choices in a self-conscious and informed way.

In constrained environments, people's decision-making can be marginalized in most aspects of life.

Then, the continuous improvement of human wellbeing is the most important common denominator of human behavior that also characterizes all economic behaviors. In Figure 3.1 human wellbeing is shown as both an outcome and a process.

Figure 3.1 Continuous improvement of human wellbeing.
Source: Pouw & McGregor (2014).

People can pursue different dimensions of human wellbeing at the same time, or prioritize one or two above others. In these instances, complex trade-offs are made. Here both objective and subjective evaluations play a critical role in the trade-offs.

Figure 3.2 illustrates how the three dimensions of wellbeing intersect. A Venn diagram helps to operationalize the abstract concept of human wellbeing. Aside from trade-offs between different wellbeing dimensions, a person can also trade off with other individuals in new forms of collective wellbeing – e.g. group well-being, organizational wellbeing, or at a national level in Gross National Happiness indexes (Lepeley, 2017a). People also experience wellbeing trade-offs over time with respect to themselves or others involved in the process.

Figure 3.2 shows multiple wellbeing intersections, where the mathematical sign ∩ stands for 'intersection', meaning that this is an area where two or more wellbeing dimensions converge: e.g. between material and relational (MR), and between material and subjective (M∩S), between relational and subjective (R∩S), and finally between all three dimensions of wellbeing (M∩R∩S), where these intersections can be positive, negative, or neutral. In the case of a positive intersection, between material and relational, this means that material aspects of wellbeing (e.g. stable income growth) reinforce relational aspects of wellbeing (e.g. broadening the professional network), leading to a multiplier effect.

In the negative case, there is a diminishing or undermining effect of one aspect of wellbeing on the other – for example, income growth at the expense of family

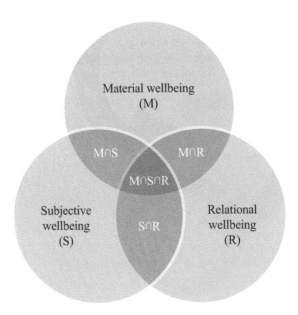

Figure 3.2 The intersection of the three dimensions of wellbeing.

Source: Pouw & McGregor (2014).

relations, leading to potential future income losses. Another example would be a diminishing effect of subjective wellbeing on material wellbeing, by means of an undesirable career shift that enhances income but not happiness.

This notion of human wellbeing makes the behavioral analysis more complex but has the advantage of providing a more realistic theory of the human being as a *social being under the assumption that* people depend on others, in life and in the working environment, to survive, and a person benefits from balancing the different wellbeing dimensions. When this interdependency is considered a starting point, instead of an end, as frequently happens in economic and organizational studies, then social inclusion and sustainability become natural events in human and organizational development leading to progress.

Elinor Ostrom explained that societies would cease to exist if they were populated only by egocentric maximizing individuals (2010). Hence putting human wellbeing at the center of economic concerns is important for economics and management relevance as social sciences able to confront disturbances of current global problems.

Organizations and human wellbeing: zooming in on economic wellbeing

Formal and informal organizations, for profit or non-profit, public or private, form an important category of multiple resources in the economy engaged in solving economic problems. As such, organizations are resource agents that make decisions about allocating resources to production, consumption, and distribution processes.

A common denominator in all organizations is that human beings constitute the core and are the collective decision-makers who command resources, functions, and processes. People and their wellbeing are the core of all organizations.

Sustainable organizations aim to organize collective activity in environmentally friendly, healthy, and safe ways (Welford & Jones, 1998; Fischer, 2010; Soyka, 2012), and produce and promote social responsibility (Lepeley *et al.*, 2016; Welford, 2013).

Regardless of the goals pursued, the wellbeing of people working within the organization is instrumental in achieving organizational sustainability. This is what Douglas McGregor refers to as "the human side of enterprise" (McGregor, 2006), and human wellbeing and organizational wellbeing must be achieved simultaneously to attain quality standards (Lepeley *et al.*, 2016; Lepeley, 2017).

People working in an organization rarely do so exclusively for income and survival reasons, but may pursue other wellbeing priorities at the same time:

1. People derive an income and other material benefits from working for an organization (M).
2. People can access knowledge and resources through the organization (M).
3. People can develop capabilities and skills in organizations. (M∩R).
4. People can access and interact with professional networks of people and other organizations (M∩R).

5. People feel part of a collective sharing an organizational identity and a set of shared values and goals (R∩S).
6. People derive a sense of stability and security working for an organization (S).
7. People derive satisfaction from performing well at work and work motivation (S).
8. People can participate in certain forms of collective decision-making and feel empowered (R∩S).

These wellbeing priorities relate to "economic wellbeing" defined as the command people have over resources and relations to fulfil needs and wants (Pouw, 2017).

In a context of limited resources and relations, in absolute and relative senses, people need to strike a balance when considering their unlimited needs and wants. This constitutes the economic problem in a nutshell. Economic wellbeing is thus a slightly narrower concept than human wellbeing, but it is also three dimensional.

If organizations embrace the wellbeing approach, a focus on economic wellbeing would be a strategic entry-point to re-conceptualizing the sustainable organization. This needs to be done at the level of people working within and with the organization, but also at organizational level.

A multidimensional wellbeing approach that assesses how organizations can achieve economic wellbeing is accomplished by:

(i)   evaluating resource use;
(ii) evaluating organizational relations with varied stakeholders;
(iii) doing so (i) and (ii) by means of internal and external, objective and subjective evaluations.

Organizations can develop internal and external strategies to respond to the wellbeing priorities of people working in the organization as a means to enhance collective organizational performance. However, if the organizational performance criteria address "sustainability", organizations' internal strategies should seek alignment with external sustainability goals.

According to the Human Centered Management model, designed by Lepeley *et al.* (2017), internal and external strategies need to be synchronized to achieve sustainability across the board. For example, if organizational identity is environmentally unfriendly, contributing to pollution and the degradation of natural resources (-), this outcome undermines people's sharing of identity, values, and goals with the organization, causing people to leave or hide their job from others.

Likewise, if the organization interacts with an international network of sustainable organizations, this commonly expedites new professional networks of people and organizations that help attract more qualified people to work for, support, or finance the organization (+).

In order to achieve synchronization between internal and external organizational sustainability strategies, the voice and participation of people working in the

Figure 3.3 Organization-level economic wellbeing.
Source: Pouw (2017).

organization, and those involved or affected by its activities and outcomes, play a critical role.

But this situation creates management challenges, namely how to weigh different interests and values while also pursuing organizational excellence and continuity? This involves a complex and continuous balancing act (Figure 3.4) that can only be performed by organizations that provide conditions to facilitate a bottom-up, participatory process of *internal* wellbeing assessment, mirroring these in *external* wellbeing assessments of the people connected with the organization (clientele, customers, users, funders, governors, and community dwellers using shared spaces or resources). It requires critical self-reflection, holding pre-defined assumptions to light in the eyes of the beholders, finding alignment between different cultures and values, and learning and adapting McGregor's words (2011) of "living well together" to an organizational environment.

The creation of a bottom-up and participatory organizational process geared at organizational sustainability and quality management is important because it is the only way in which "inter-subjectivity" (Pouw *et al.*, 2016) between the internal and external organization can emerge. Inter-subjectivity means that people collectively agree on the definition of a problem, and a shared set of interests and values. It comes out of group discussions or group processes. But before agreement can be reached, *human interaction* is needed at multiple levels of the internal and external organization, from the bottom up to higher levels so that capacity building can take place, and wellbeing concerns and priorities at the bottom can inform agenda setting at the top.

Figure 3.4 Balancing internal and external human wellbeing.
Source: Author.

Otherwise, the balancing act remains one of management navigating back and forth between multiple, and often disconnected, subjectivities that may never converge. Inter-subjectivity can lead to new understandings and knowledge of a situation and comprehensive problem perception, which can create a greater feeling of ownership and responsibility, and more funding and support for an organizational strategy or decision.

I am drawing this lesson from our participatory evaluation of development interventions in different countries in Africa, where we found that development actors, including public and private organizations, are allowed to make mistakes in the communities where they implement their interventions, but only as long as they keep an open door policy to always consult with local communities first, maintain a long-term presence, be open for critique and consultation, correct mistakes, and be transparent and honest about commitments (Pouw *et al.*, 2016). Sustainable organizations manage internal and external human interactions well, taking a bottom-up and participatory approach that will unleash transformative change in organizations.

Concluding remarks

The concept of human wellbeing distinguishes between material, relational, and subjective wellbeing. It looks into how people as social human beings live well together, instead of focusing on how individuals live well by maximizing individual gains.

For organizations committed to organizational sustainability, the focused economic wellbeing concept can be achieved by holding internal and external strategies for sustainability that promote human centered approaches as a necessary condition to attain success and the continuous improvement necessary in quality management.

Establishing human interactions at multiple levels of the internal and external organizational environment in a bottom-up and participatory manner enables organizations to achieve transformative change.

With inter-subjective learning, capacities are built, knowledge and values are shared, and new directions for organizational sustainability emerge.

Furthermore, internal and external organizational environments are subject to changes and shocks, often unforeseen. So how can organizations adapt to changes and shocks while improving human and economic wellbeing that warrant organizational sustainability is a constant inquiry.

Different case studies of organizations exposed to various shocks help to shed light on these complex dynamics.

Last but not least, discourses on "sustainability" are themselves subject to change. So organizations need to be aware and informed about changes in discourses as a matter of strategic concern because clashes between "old" and "new" discourses may negatively impact an organization's performance and success. How can organizations continue to be knowledgeable about new sustainability discourses without getting off course? This is the final question all organizations need to address.

References

Bardy, R., & Massaro, M. (2012). A stimulus for sustainable growth and development: Construing a composite index to measure overall corporate performance. *Journal of Organisational Transformation & Social Change, 9*(2), 155–174.

Deneulin, S., & McGregor, J.A. (2010). The Capability Approach and the Politics of a Social Conception of Wellbeing. *European Journal of Social Theory, 13*(4), 501–519.

Kourula, A., Pisani, N., & Kolk, A. (2017). Corporate sustainability and inclusive development: highlights from international business and management research. *Current Opinion in Environmental Sustainability, 24*, 14–18.

Lepeley, M.T., Pizarro, O., & Mandakovic, V. (2015). Women entrepreneurs in Chile: Three decades of challenges and lessons in innovation and business sustainability. *Female Entrepreneurship in Transition Economies: Trends and Challenges, 247.*

Lepeley, M.T., von Kimakowitz, E., & Bardy, R. (Eds.). (2016). *Human Centered Management in executive education: Global imperatives, innovation and new directions.* Basingstoke, UK: Palgrave.

Lepeley, M.T. (2017a). Bhutan's Gross National Happiness: An approach to human centred sustainable development. *South Asian Journal of Human Resources Management, 4*(2), 1–11.

Lepeley, M.T. (2017b). *Human Centered Management: The 5 Pillars of Organizational Quality and Global Sustainability.* Oxford, UK: Routledge.

Likoko, E., & Kini, J. (2017). Inclusive business: A business approach to development. *Current Opinion in Environmental Sustainability, 24*, 84–88.

McGregor, D. (2006). *The human side of enterprise.* New York: McGraw Hill.

McGregor, J.A. (2011). Facing the challenge of living well together. *The Broker.* www.thebrokeronline.eu/Articles/Facing-the-challenge-of-living-well-together

McGregor, J.A., & Pouw, N. (2016). Towards an economics of well-being. *Cambridge Journal of Economics, 41*(4), 1123–1142.

Ostrom, E. (2010). Beyond markets and states: polycentric governance of complex economic systems. *Transnational Corporations Review, 2*(2), 1–12.

Ostrom, E., & Williamson, O.E. (2000). Elinor Ostrom. *Public Choice: A Different Approach to the Study of Public Administration, 31*(2).

Pouw, N. (2017). *Introduction to Gender and Wellbeing in Microeconomics.* London and New York: Routledge.

Pouw, N., Dietz, T., Bélemvire, A., de Groot, D., Millar, D., Obeng, F., . . . & Zaal, F. (2016). Participatory assessment of development interventions: Lessons learned from a new evaluation methodology in Ghana and Burkina Faso. *American Journal of Evaluation, 38*(1), 47–59.

Pouw, N., & McGregor, A. (2014). An Economics of Wellbeing: What would economics look like if it were focused on human wellbeing? *IDS Working Papers, 2014*(436), 1–27.

Soyka, P. A. (2012). *Creating a sustainable organization: Approaches for enhancing corporate value through sustainability.* Upper Saddle River, NJ: Pearson Education.

Welford, R., & Jones, D. (1998). Beyond environmentalism and towards the sustainable organization. In R. Welford (Ed.), *Corporate Environmental Management 1–Systems and Strategies* (pp. 237–257). London: Earthscan.

Welford, R. (2013). *Hijacking environmentalism: Corporate responses to sustainable development.* Routledge.

Part II
Wellbeing and work

4 Quality of Work Life in Brazil

Mário César Ferreira

Introduction

Quality of Work Life (QWL) is an increasingly common interest around the world, especially in corporate settings. A recent Google search for the keywords "quality of work life" in Portuguese, Spanish, Italian, French, and English revealed close to a billion results. The entry in English alone offered 798 million links to the topic and variants of it, confirming that QWL is a pressing concern on the agenda of leaders, managers, workers, researchers, and government officials.

But what are the reasons behind the growing QWL argument in the corporate sector? This discussion is important because a good understanding of these reasons provides the essential foundation for the improvement of organizational practices and work management, which will be described in this chapter using Brazil as a reference.

A review of the literature on labor and health science focused on Organizational and Work Psychology and Administration and on technical and government reports shows three groups of interdependent factors that merge to shape growing interest on QWL. They can be summarized as follows:

- The first group is concerned with the ongoing productive restructuring process that, since 1965 to 1975, has been supported by the New Information and Communication Technologies (NICT). The latter are significantly and rapidly changing working conditions, the nature of tasks, interaction between people, organizational structures, and labor management (Leite, 2003; Castel, 2003; Baumgarten & Holzmann, 2011). Ongoing change is demanding new forms of recruitment, selection, and training in organizations in higher synchrony with emerging worker profiles. In this sphere, the main challenges are how to drive the process of rapid change with assertiveness and, in particular, preventing negative effects in the production of goods and services, such as errors, rework, performance declines, reduced productivity, material loss, and equipment damage.
- The second group derives from evidence that problems with the production of goods and services may inflict costs for workers. Restructuring processes can result in negative occupational health and safety outcomes, such as accidents, psychosocial risks, stress, burnout syndrome, mental disorders,

and occupational diseases. Such outcomes have a high potential to exacerbate production problems, increasing negative effects, such as workers' leave due to injuries, sickness, and higher risk levels associated with production processes. Therefore, the competitive capacity of private corporations and the quality of public services provided to citizens are threatened. Two International Labor Organization reports (OIT, 2013; ILO, 2016) provide a global view of accident and occupational disease rates that highlight the importance of psychosocial risks produced by work-related stress. These reports illustrate the extent and severity of the problems in this second group of factors.

- The third group is a combination of the previous groups. Problems in production and employee health and safety inevitably impact the private sector customer, consumer, or citizen, or the public sector consumer levels of satisfaction. In the private sector, problems with production have a high potential to put at risk and disrupt coveted consumer loyalty. In the public sector, it impairs the practice of citizenship by limiting access to guaranteed rights, which are threatened by complaints to consumer protection agencies in the form of grievances or protests.

Based on this background, Quality of Work Life (QWL) has risen as an urgent need and a real alternative to meet the challenges of the negative impacts of productive restructuring processes, in particular those aiming to promote an equitable, sustainable, and socially inclusive global economy.

In the human-centered Era of Knowledge and Information, it is imperative to change the paradigm of prevailing conceptions that view workers as "resources" and citizens as "voracious protesters." Today it is vital to bring workers' needs and citizens' demands, abilities, and expectations to the foreground as central organizational priorities in the private and public sectors.

On the threshold of the twenty-first century, new technologies, connectivity, rapid changes, and uncertainty are key factors of the complexity that disrupts organizations and influences new ways of working, living, and participating in organizations (Lepeley, 2017). Therefore, high awareness of the QWL of people who work in organizations is a fundamental, strategic, and unavoidable challenge in improvementinghuman centered management models (Lepeley, 2017).

Creativity, the ability to work effectively, and human talent are essential elements for achieving equitable, sustainable, and socially inclusive workplaces. Finally, the focus of human centered management – which values human capital, talent, and knowledge – is inseparable from the promotion of QWL in organizational contexts. In this light, the assumption is to prepare meet the wellbeing of people's customers, managers, workers, and suppliers. In other words, attaining wellbeing standards is the new imperative for governments, companies, directors, managers, workers, and customers.

World recognized quality standards and QWL are a global and collective endeavor where everybody (governments, companies, directors, managers, workers, and customers) must share responsibility.

To achieve this global objective, it is necessary to start clarifying what Quality of Work Life (QWL) is from the perspective of workers, organizations, and society. What are the main variables that provide a framework for QWL? What is the focus of QWL studies? Familiarity with the latest research and results is not only essential for the construction of a critical view of QWL, but also to conduct projects that lead to the improvement of organizational contexts. Moreover, this would allow better understanding of how quality of life practices in public and private organizations are characterized.

Quality of Work Life background

Although the interest of corporations in QWL has increased considerably in the last 20 years, its importance in scientific research has not received comparable attention. From the academic point of view, QWL is not, strictly speaking, a new topic of interest. In fact, its emergence is estimated to coincide with the beginning of the restructuring process between 1965 and 1975.

This evidence shows that, for half a century, QWL studies have been anchored in a research construct that is focused on identification of QWL elements and the procedures commonly used for measurement. Approaches that apply theoretical models and research analysis to public and private organizations.

Among QWL pioneers are the works of Walton (1973), Hackman and Oldham (1975), and Westley (1979). Since the 1990s, scientific study of QWL has grown with the work of Lawler (1982), Mirvis and Lawler (1984), Baba and Jamal (1991), Albuquerque and França (1998), Lacaz (2000), Ellis and Pompli (2002), Bearfield (2003), Martel and Dupuis (2006), Ferreira, Alves, and Tostes (2009), Bagtasos (2011), Ferreira, Ferreira, Paschoal, and Almeida (2014), Almeida, Ferreira, and Brusiquese (2015), and Verma and Monga (2015).

A descriptive and exploratory analysis of the most researched QWL components classifies them into five groups that were proposed by Ferreira (2012). These essential QWL components are shown in Table 4.1.

A distinctive feature of QWL studies is the diversity of variables considered by different authors. Among the 48 positive and negative indicators identified in Table 4.1, the most important are those related to task design, participation, and autonomy. Overall, these are indicators of labor management models. The socioeconomic relations in corporate contexts and the perspective of professional growth appear in second and third place, respectively. Surprisingly, aspects related to work conditions are in last place.

Taken together, these frameworks point to organization and labor management as key factors that influence QWL studies.

QWL approaches emphasize: intrinsic and extrinsic aspects of work, motivation, working conditions, psychological needs; work routines, job satisfaction and commitment; and happiness and life satisfaction. These variables fluctuate according to types of organizations and variety of work teams.

Researchers emphasize different aspects. Some focus on work-related contexts and the workplace; others on psychological factors, such as personality, perceptions of happiness, and life satisfaction.

Table 4.1 Interest factors and variables in Quality of Work Life (QWL).

Factors	Variables	
Work organization (n = 17)	• Job autonomy • Employee participation in decision-making • Additional work activities • Rigid/inflexible work organization • Autonomy in task execution • Job responsibilities • Job requirements • Degree of involvement in decision-making	• Responsibility • Shiftwork • Skill variety • Task identity • Work role ambiguity • Work role conflict • Workload
Social and professional relations (n = 9)	• Climate • Cooperation • Feedback • Interpersonal relationships • Relationships with supervisor/peers	• Professional isolation • Interpersonal conflict • Social support • Ways of controlling
Growth and professional development (n = 9)	• Equal employment opportunities • Equity • Meaningful futures at work • Opportunities for advancement • Opportunities to learn and grow	• Opportunity to learn new skills • Personal development • Professional development • Training • Use of one's skills
Work Recognition (n = 7)	• Compensation • Equitable wages • Fairness • Job security	• Recognition at work • Rewards • Social relevance of work or product
Working Conditions (n = 6)	• Adequacy of resources • Ancillary programs • Facilities	• Safe work environment • Working conditions

Source: Author.

Interest in instruments to measure QWL has increased significantly in the scientific literature (Sirgy, Efraty, Siegel & Lee, 2001; Worrall & Cooper, 2006; Edwards, Van Laar, Easton, & Van Laar, 2009; Devappa, Nanjundeswaraswamy, & Rashmi, 2015). This dimension exhibits a hegemonic tendency of quantitative designs with predominant use of psychometric scales to evaluate employee perceptions of QWL and correlations with demographic variables and professional profiles.

An assessment of QWL literature reveals some limits and problems that must be overcome for effective human centered management in organizations. These limitations highlight the academic side of a hegemonic approach to QWL from two dimensions:

• Lack of consensus regarding a definition of QWL as a concept of scientific inquiry. In some cases, QWL is taken as self-explanatory. Different authors identify QWL components, describe its characteristics, and show correlations between variables associated with it, but in general fail to formulate a concrete concept of QWL. However, after interpreting different QWL approaches, it is possible to figure out that an employee's wellbeing is the common denominator among different perspectives. The two aspects of concern that guide hegemonic approaches are "organizations" and "productivity." The most typical indicators included are: task identity, organizational climate, job training, and rewards, and these are implicitly subordinated to productivity and organizational objectives. The concern for job satisfaction is used as a pretext to boost productivity and the employees' commitment to the organization. Hence, productivity issues are associated with utilitarian pragmatism, deviating from their main role as drivers of health and wellbeing at work.

- There is an underlying conception of "individual, work, and organization" in the academic hegemonic approach to QWL. A feature that cuts across this approach is to treat this triad as a single object, where "people and work" are subordinated to other organizational imperatives. In this scenario, a role reversal takes place: people and their productive activities are at the service of organizations, not the opposite, as would be recommended to meet the fundamental principles of human centered management (Lepeley, 2017).

In addition to these limitations, two other characteristics of the QWL academic hegemonic approach present additional challenges.

Among the main concerns of these models is that they are remarkably difficult to implement in corporate contexts; additionally, there are ethical implications for people, organizations, and society. Under these conditions, even a poor and reductionist academic design has the potential to gain visibility. For example, the production of knowledge is self-generated and not designed to fulfil human needs in the real world. In fact, such models constitute a form of research practice that transforms organizations into a kind of "laboratory" merely to collect data and test hypotheses. Once the knowledge is produced, the "research" objective is satisfied.

The other has to do with a relatively distant scientific production, isolated from what is happening in the workplace. The production of knowledge is restricted within the organization's walls, isolated form the community and the external environment. The results are not discussed clearly or integrated with other organizations.

Organizations – namely units of the corporate environment, which also serve as a place to conduct research – are paradoxically single and isolated units. This is as if a part were separated from the whole without any intent for analytical return.

The result is the production of a type of scientific knowledge that is alienated, restricted, and almost incommunicable. This characteristic goes against the current objectives of scientific production based on solutions for global problems that must be confronted by people, the economy, and society in general.

QWL scientific production needs to be associated with and to interact with other organizations in an increasingly interconnected world, a sustainable economy, and societies that are truly inclusive.

Quality of Work Life: a brief overview of practices in Brazilian organizations

An analysis of the QWL scientific hegemonic production and the application of QWL practices in public and private organizations reveals the gap between the knowledge generated in QWL research institutions and the reality in organizations. This is the case in Brazil, the seventh largest economy in the world today.

Brazilian researchers (Ferreira Alves & Tostes, 2009; Ferreira, Almeida Guimarães & Wargas, 2011) identify a set of palliative QWL practices applied in some organizations. Table 4.2 illustrates the most common types of services and practices (actions) in Brazilian public and private organizations.

Table 4.2 Types of services and examples of QWL practices.

Types of Services	Examples of QWL practices	Types of services	Examples of QWL practices
Psychological support	• Self-knowledge • Meditation • Stress management • Astrology chart	Culture and leisure activities	• Choir • Parties • Ballroom dancing and rhythms • Going out
Physical support	• Posture controller • Ergonomic blitz • Labor gymnastics • Walking and running groups	Corporate support	• Health call center • Corporate fitness • Anti-stress rooms • Absenteeism tracking
Body-mind therapies	• Labor kinesiotherapy • Aromatherapy • Geochromotherapy • Alchemical flower therapy	Diagnoses	• Assessment of weight gain/loss • Physical assessment • Lifestyle mapping • Biometric screenings
"Eastern Holistic" approaches	• Ayurvedic massage • Shiatsu • Tai Chi Chuan • Labor Yoga	Programs	• Anti-smoking program • Program to reduce sedentary behavior • Drug treatment program • Corporate volunteer programs
Nutritional re-education	• Healthy eating • Individual counseling to gain/lose weight • Control of risk factors • Personalized nutritional guidance		

Source: Ferreira (2015a).

In general, these services and practices show the prevailing palliative and hegemonic approach of QWL in Brazilian organizations. They are distant from the human centered management paradigm and can be considered a palliative for three main reasons:

- Such approaches transfer QWL responsibility from the organization to workers. Organizational sources of distress and fatigue remain untouched, and employees are taken as the flexible component, meaning that they should adjust and adapt to even hostile corporate environments. It is inaccurate to assume that these organizational approaches increase employees' physical and mental strength to tackle organizational adversity, which is commonly considered a natural outcome. Here, flexibility, wrongly understood as the practical approach in organizational management, is embedded in each employee (Sennett, 2001). This is a misunderstanding of resilience as exclusively related to organizations, ignoring that organizations only become resilient when the people who work in the organization make it possible (Lepeley, 2017).
- QWL practices are compensatory to fight the distressing experiences of employees in the corporate context while intending to discover and deploy effective solutions to solve organizational climate challenges that impair daily work life. Although some general practices may be beneficial to improve the employees' lifestyle, such as healthy eating, many are inconsistent with deeper causes of problems arising from work situations. In this case, the palliative character of QWL actions is critical.
- Hegemonic QWL practices aim to ensure productivity rates, which are vital elements for continuous improvement in organizational management. This includes the efforts companies make to stimulate employees' proactive participation, absenteeism avoidance, accident prevention and avoidance, and promotion of good health. Organizational objectives and goals need to be clearly targeted for high achievement within the cost–benefit ratios contingent with organizational planning. Organizational management practices and work practices remain unquestionably taboo topics. This perspective on productivity departs from its healthy dimension, which is, nevertheless, a concept that truly promotes wellbeing at work.

A close examination of this hegemonic QWL approach can be compared with an internal corporate marketing strategy. This can be labeled as a "mind-body restoration" QWL strategy for the target audience of workers (Ferreira *et al.*, 2011). Such a QWL activity also reveals the existence of a diverse and fruitful market of companies that sell QWL services where customers are quite attracted by the products offered. Emphasizing productivity means that companies develop advertising campaigns focused on "corporate health," "organizational wellbeing," "occupational health," "business needs," "cost optimization," "results maximization," and "partner profits."

In close synchrony with the needs of individuals, the emphasis of corporate speech supports "stress management," "emotional health care," "development of anti-stress environments," and "immersion in cultural and leisure activities." This QWL approach strengthens effective resource for businesses to deal with endemic problems of absenteeism, lack of motivation, and job rotation.

Furthermore, the QWL approach is in line with the models of organizational and work management aimed at capturing employees' interest in accruing benefits of high personal performance as a mechanism for productivity in the corporate context, as identified by Antunes and Alves (2004). The approach is aligned with organizational management models that promote work autonomy and decision-making capacity, together with greater responsibility for results and areas of improvement, and risk taking at the individual level, which is essential for creativity and innovation in the Brazilian work scenario, where fear of unemployment and casualization of formal working relations coexist. These elements adhere to the conception of a world of work that is guided by the cult of performance (Ehrenberg, 2000) and, at the same time, by the prospect of promoting one's own professional life (Gaulejac, 2007). Here, unlike the human centered management approach proposed by Lepeley (2017), problems are not treated as challenges and steps towards continuous and sustainable organizational improvement are taken.

In summary, this QWL approach (which seems to be more like a "body–mind restoration" type) is presented as a solution to manage the negative impacts of the economic transformations, especially regarding employee health and safety. In fact, such QWL practices are nothing more than ways of imposing employee submission to the imperatives of productivity. In this view, maximizing productivity remains a central goal and, as far as QWL is concerned, the emphasis is on transferring the responsibility for its promotion to the individual.

Activity-Centered Ergonomics Applied to the Quality of Work Life (AEA_QWL) Model that benefits workers, organizations, and society

Overcoming the reductionist and palliative QWL approach – as seen in Brazilian organizations – and moving towards the implementation of human centered management is a significant challenge. On this topic and for over a decade, a series of studies (Ferreira, 2008; Ferreira, 2011; Ferreira, 2012, Ferreira, 2015b) has been conducted at the University of Brasilia (Brazil) resulting in the formulation of an approach (still under construction) called Activity-Centered Ergonomics Applied to Quality of Work Life (AEA_QWL).

The QWL is proposed to provide support to managers and organizations seeking to restructure practices under the umbrella of the human centered management paradigm. This approach defines QWL, its theoretical and methodological assumptions, and its main characteristics, and also reveals concrete results obtained in Brazilian organizations.

The QWL concept for the AEA_QWL dimension is built on empirical research as follows:

> From the perspective of organizations, QWL is an organizational management model structured on a set of norms, guidelines, and practices defined by working conditions and socio-professional relationships. The main goal is the promotion of individual and collective wellbeing, anchored in personal development of workers and organizational citizenship in the workplace. From the perspective of workers, QWL is expressed through general and specific perceptions (organizational context and working conditions, respectively), based on: work experiences conducting to wellbeing, institutional and collective recognition, possibility for professional growth, and respect for individual characteristics.
>
> (Ferreira, 2012, p. 172)

QWL combines two complementary dimensions: a macro organizational framework, designed as a management model, and a collective realm of people and their perceptions. This is the conceptual framework of QWL under the following methodological assumptions:

- A survey of workers' perceptions about QWL in the workplace is the central paradigm for this approach. This is essential in developing a transformational intervention model to promote QWL sustainability over time and to deter the traditional and obsolete palliative approach mentioned before. QWL action plans should be developed based on the "desire" of most workers to develop an inclusive collective construction that can effectively address the needs and expectations of all the people who work in the organization.
- The starting point for this study is the assessment of QWL in organizations. It is based on diagnoses conducted with scientific rigor that include macro and micro diagnostic features, multi-method research, and quail-quantitative analysis. In order to attain continuous improvement and reach quality standards, the assessment procedure must effectively demonstrate active participation of the target group during all stages of the analysis, and especially during the process of dissemination and validation of the findings. In this process, the participation of professionals from different areas of knowledge facilitates a multidisciplinary debate that integrates different perspectives of analysis, knowledge, and talents.
- An ethical commitment of respect for human beings guides the implementation of the AEA_QWL approach. This commitment should be shared among participants, ensuring judicious respect to all in relation to the following assumptions: (a) voluntary participation, (b) confidentiality in handling the personal information of participants at all stages of the research, and (c) guarantee of anonymity in the dissemination of diagnostic results.
- AEA_QWL interventions are not neutral. They can serve or act against interests present in the organization. It is necessary to develop general

awareness that this procedure is deployed in a possibly conflicting, ambiguous, and complex traditional process-centered (as opposed to human centered) organizational setting, integrated by a variety of people in different roles, with different needs, expectations, values, beliefs, and interests. Thus, in addition to the scientific and ethical dimensions that guide the AEA_QWL approach, researchers must be acutely aware of the way they conduct the approach; the assessment instruments used; and securing respect for diversity in organizations and corporate cultures. Establishing dialogues, holding consultations, and, above all, building consensus are permanent strategic challenges, but they are essential for successful deployment.

Moreover, in relation to its methodology, by operating at two complementary analytical levels (macro and micro diagnostics), AEA_QWL relies on the use of two interdependent instrumental resources.

- At the macro level, diagnosis is conducted based on the application of the Quality of Work Life Assessment Questionnaire (QWL_AQ). This tool is divided into two complementary parts: (a) a quantitative part consisting of an 11-point Likert scale organized in four sections (workplace, work management, work-related distress, and positive and negative affection) composed of 63 items; (b) a qualitative part consisting of four open-ended questions to capture respondents' opinions on the following items: perceptions leading to a concrete definition of a QWL concept, identification of sources of wellbeing and ill-being at work, and comments and suggestions for continuous improvement of QWL. Quantitative data are interpreted with SPSS software using descriptive and inferential analyses. Qualitative data, in turn, are analyzed with the free online software IRaMuTeQ.
- At the micro level, the diagnosis is intended to improve results obtained at the macro level and to give a close look at specific topics to understand the origin, dynamics, and features of positive or negative aspects, using the Ergonomic Work Analysis tool (EWA). In this case, the evaluation instruments used are: semi-structured interviews, focus group, free and systematic observation, and measurement of physical and environmental variables, such as acoustic comfort, visual comfort, and thermal comfort.
- There are also two open-ended questions that integrate QWL_AQ – they aim to investigate: (a) the respondent's degree of intention to leave the job; and (b) cases of sick leave due to work-related health problems.

The psychometric method used to assess the quantitative results of the QWL_AQ reveals three complementary levels of QWL indicators: negative, positive, and neutral. Therefore, a QLW approach captures negative aspects that affect organizations and require particular attention for improvement, as well as neutral and positive positions of the participants surveyed. What is positive, for example, needs to be preserved and constantly improved to attain organizational sustainability.

The process of improvement, maturity, and reliability of the AEA_QWL approach is reflected in its adoption by 30 Brazilian public organizations in the last decade.

The realization of the approach includes three stages: (a) macro and micro QWL diagnoses; (b) formulation of QWL policy based on results from the diagnostic assessment: conceptual framework, normative basis, values; and (c) a QWL collaboration plan detailing projects and actions in the short, medium, and long term.

Consolidated results have shown that the main sources of discomfort at work are associated with: (a) poor work conditions, (b) lack of respect for the human needs of employees in the organization, (c) conflicting social and professional relationships, (d) lack of recognition and rewards at work, (e) little or no prospect for professional growth, and (f) difficulties reconciling work demands with private life.

The implementation of this QWL helps organizations to evaluate organizational structure and strategies aiming to deploy a human-centered management culture that strengthens social ties and improves working conditions through planning, implementation, and rigorous assessment of projects directed towards the continuous improvement of QWL and productivity in organizations.

Deployment of the QWL model is consistent with the challenges of the ever-changing world and workforce that shape globalization. The importance, consequences, and implications of QWL deployment are not restricted to the walls of the organization, but should be associated with a comprehensive scope of principles and practices aimed at rescuing the human meaning of work and strengthening socially responsible and inclusive organizations.

Therefore, in addition to the arguments presented throughout this chapter, it is time to answer the question embedded in the title of this chapter. QWL is closely aligned with the needs and interests of workers in general, and the fact that an organization's employees can rescue the human meaning of work has great potential to effectively synchronize the individual and social identities necessary to reach high productivity as a permanent source of people's wellbeing.

The quality of work life that expedites continuous improvement in organizations in Brazil and the world is built on a framework that contributes to their trans-formation into useful, inclusive, and sustainable social instruments. The quality of work life that truly matters to society is the one that helps people to live in a peaceful and cooperative work environment.

References

Albuquerque, L.G., & França, A.C.L. (1998). Estratégias de recursos humanos e gestão da qualidade de vida no trabalho: o stress e a expansão do conceito de qualidade total. *Revista de Administração, 33*, 40–51.

Almeida, J.G., Ferreira, M.C., & Brusiquese, R.G. (2015). Between heaven and hell: The importance of interpersonal relations at work to quality of work life perception. *Business Management Review* (BMR), *4*, 390–400.

Antunes, R., & Alves, G. (2004). As mutações no mundo do trabalho na era da mundialização do capital. *Educação & Sociedade, 25,* (87), 335–351.

Baba, V.V., & Jamal, M. (1991). Routinisation of job context and job content as related to employees' quality of working life: A study of psychiatric nurses. *Journal of Organisational Behaviour, 12,* 379–386.

Bagtasos, M. R. (2011). Quality of work life: A review of literature. *Business & Economics Review, 20,* 1–8.

Baumgarten, M., & Holzmann, L. (2011). Reestruturação produtiva. In A.D. Cattani and L. Holzmann (Eds.). *Dicionário de Trabalho e Tecnologia.* Porto Alegre, Brazil: Zouk, 315–319.

Bearfield, S. (2003). *Quality of Working Life.* Aciirt Working paper 86. University of Sydney. www.acirrt.com

Castel, R. (2003). *As metamorfoses da questão social: Uma crônica do salário.* Petrópolis, RJ: Vozes.

Devappa, R.S., Nanjundeswaraswamy, T.S., & Rashmi, S. (2015). Quality of work life: Scale development and validation. *International Journal of Caring Sciences, 8*(2), 281–300.

Edwards, J., Van Laar, D.L., & Easton, S. (2009). The Work-Related Quality of Life (WRQoL) scale for higher education employees. *Quality in Higher Education, 15*(3), 207–219.

Ehrenberg, A. (2000). *La fatigue d'être soi. Dépression et société.* Paris: Éditions Odile Jacob.

Ellis, N., & Pompli, A. (2002). *Quality of working life for nurses.* Commonwealth Department of Health and Ageing, Canberra.

Ferreira, M.C. (2008). A ergonomia da atividade se interessa pela qualidade de vida no trabalho? Reflexões empíricas e teóricas. *Cadernos de Psicologia Social do Trabalho* (USP), *11,* 83–99.

Ferreira, M.C. (2011). A ergonomia da atividade pode promover a qualidade de vida no trabalho? Reflexões de natureza metodológica. *Revista Psicologia: Organizações e Trabalho, 11,* 8–20.

Ferreira, M.C. (2012). *Qualidade de Vida no Trabalho. Uma Abordagem Centrada no Olhar dos Trabalhadores.* Brasília, Brazil: Paralelo 15, 2ª edição revista e ampliada.

Ferreira, M.C. (2015a). Qualidade de Vida no Trabalho (QVT): Do assistencialismo à promoção efetiva. *Laboreal* (Porto Online), *11,* 28–35.

Ferreira, M.C. (2015b). Ergonomia da atividade aplicada à qualidade de vida no trabalho: Lugar, importância e contribuição da Análise Ergonômica do Trabalho (AET). *Revista Brasileira de Saúde Ocupacional, 40,* 18–29.

Ferreira, M.C., Almeida, C.P., Guimarães, M.C., & Wargas, R.D. (2011). Qualidade de Vida no Trabalho: A ótica da restauração corpo-mente e o olhar dos trabalhadores. In M.C. Ferreira, J.N.G. Araújo, C.P. Almeida, & A.M. Mendes (Eds.), *Dominação e Resistência no Contexto Trabalho-Saúde.* São Paulo, Brazil: Editora Mackenzie, 159–182.

Ferreira, M.C., Alves, L., & Tostes, N. (2009). Gestão de qualidade de vida no trabalho (QVT) no serviço público federal: O descompasso entre problemas e práticas gerenciais. *Psicologia: Teoria e Pesquisa, 25,* 319–327.

Ferreira, R. R., Ferreira, M. C., Paschoal, T., & Almeida, J. G. (2014). Perceptions of Quality of Work Life (QWL), labor management practices and well-being: A inferential study in a Brazilian IT company. In *28th International Congress of Applied Psychology,* Paris: ICAP, 1–1.

Gaulejac, V. (2007) *Gestão como doença social: Ideologia, poder gerencialista e fragmentação social*. São Paulo, Brazil: Ideias e Letras.

Hackman, J. R., & Oldham, G. R. (1975). Development of the Job Diagnostic Survey. *Journal of Applied Psychology*, *60*(2), 159–170.

ILO International Labour Office (2016). *Work place stress. A collective challenge*. www.ilo.org/safework/info/publications/WCMS_466547/lang—en/index.htm

Lacaz, F.A.C. (2000). Qualidade de vida no trabalho e saúde/doença. *Ciência & Saúde Coletiva*, *5*, 151–161.

Lawler, E.E. (1982). Strategies for improving the quality of work life. *American Psychologist*, 37, 2005, 486–493.

Leite, M.P. (2003). *Trabalho e sociedade em transformação: Mudanças produtivas e atores sociais*. São Paulo, Brazil: Fundação Perseu Abramo.

Lepeley, M.T. (2017). *Human Centered Management. The Five Pillars of Quality Organizations and Global Sustainability*. Saltaire, UK: Greenleaf.

Martel, J.P., & Dupuis, G. (2006). Quality of work life: Theoretical and methodological problems, and presentation of a new model and measuring instrument. *Social Indicators Research*, 77, 333–368.

Mirvis, P.H., & Lawler, E.E. (1984). Accounting for the Quality of Work Life. *Journal of Occupational Behaviour*, 5, 197–212.

OIT Organización Internacional del Trabajo. (2013). *La prevención de las enfermedades profesionales*. Genebra, first edition.

Sennett, R. (2001). *A corrosão do caráter: Consequências pessoais do trabalho no novo capitalismo*. Rio de Janeiro: Editora Record.

Sirgy, M.J., Efraty, D., Siegel, P., & Lee, D. (2001). A new measure of quality of work life (QoWL) based on need satisfaction and spillover theories. *Social Indicators Research*, 55, 241–302.

Verma, P., & Monga, O.P. (2015). Understanding quality of work life in contemporary world. *International Journal of Emerging Research in Management & Technology*, *4*, 149–153.

Walton, R.E. (1973). Quality of Working Life: What is it? *Sloan Management Review*, *15*(1), 11–21.

Westley, W.A. (1979). Problems and Solutions in the Quality of Working Life. *Human Relations*, *32*, 113–123.

Worrall, L., & Cooper, C.L. (2006). *The Quality of Working Life: Managers' health and well-being*. Executive Report, Chartered Management Institute.

5 Safety and employee health and wellbeing

Daniela M. Andrei, Paola Ochoa, and Mark A. Griffin

Introduction

The "Health and Safety" concept is commonly used in contemporary organizations, with both terms being more often used together than separately. Most organizations have a Health and Safety Department, or Health and Safety managers, coordinating initiatives and programs aimed at improving health and/or safety of employees. In a similar way, wider national or international organizations tend to use "health" and "safety" as inherently linked terms when devising strategies, policies, regulations, recommendations, or programs. But when analyzing both actual practice and research, it becomes apparent that, more often than not, health and safety are treated independently, and there is minimal integration between the two constructs. This is especially true when the concept of health encompasses issues of employees' mental health and wellbeing at work. For example, recent attention to mental health in the Australian mining industry has resulted in companies implementing independent safety and mental health interventions through different departments focusing on distinct goals and reporting structures.

Growing awareness that mental health is an essential component of Occupational Health and Safety (OHS), in addition to physical health, is expanding the field but also increasing risk of the further fragmentation of efforts to manage an increasingly complex domain.

Increased attention to the demands of workers in remote mining sites in Australia highlights the need to more effectively include concerns on mental illness in OHS responsibilities. But for most companies, and in particular for companies managing hazardous operations, the role of mental health is difficult to integrate with urgent priorities to reduce accidents and injuries, and even harder to align with scheduled productivity goals. It is our contention that one of the main reasons for this difficulty is related to a predominant focus on the negative aspects of employee mental health – and on individually oriented, reactive interventions to mitigate poor mental health outcomes (Caulfield, Chang, Dollard & Elshaug, 2004; Kompier, Cooper & Geurts, 2000). However, a positive approach to employee mental health improves links with a high range of organizational outcomes because it allows for a clearer focus on positive aspects of employee performance and wellbeing at work and in life.

This chapter explores how to improve integration of safety and health with each other as a necessary condition to support important individual and organizational outcomes. The focus is on wellbeing rather than purely on physical health for the following reasons: (1) research on health and safety as one field of concern seems to operationalize health almost exclusively in terms of physical health, leaving mental health issues unexplored; (2) attention to mental health in safety contexts has focused predominantly on the more negative aspects of mental health; and (3) a focus on positive aspects of employees' mental health (i.e. wellbeing) allows for better integration of safety, health, and wider organizational goals, identifying psychological mechanisms effective in supporting safe operations, and improving wellbeing and performance of employees. Therefore, although work wellbeing and health (mental and physical) are inherently linked, this chapter focuses predominantly on aspects of wellbeing at work and determinants and outcomes in relation to safety and overall individual wellbeing.

An overview of existing research linking safety and employee wellbeing facilitates the development of a framework highlighting the role of psychological mechanisms reinforcing safety behavior and employee wellbeing. In particular, active mental states based on positive affectivity (positive emotions), recovery (replenished resources), and cognitive states (self-efficacy) that empower individuals to work proactively achieving individual and organizational goals. The same mechanisms facilitate better understanding leading to health and safety practices and policies devised to contribute to employees' performance that contribute to meeting wider organizational goals.

Overview of existing evidence linking safety and employee wellbeing

Existing research provides limited support for expanding the OHS field incorporating employee wellbeing. Lack of physical harm is often indirectly implied in research focusing on safety, often as an outcome of safety practices and policies (meta-analysis conducted by Christian, Bradley, Wallace, & Burke, 2009, safety outcomes are defined in terms of accidents and injuries) or even as a broader indicator of business unit outcomes (e.g. Harter, Schmidt, & Hayes, 2002). The same applies to wellbeing. Although the interest in employee wellbeing in safety critical contexts is growing, recent publications on safety show lower number of papers linking employee wellbeing to safety specific demands and resources and safety outcomes (Nahrgang, Morgeson, & Hoffman, 2011), when compared with traditional topics of safety behaviors. A literature search using general terms revealed a limited number of studies that integrate safety and wellbeing or mental health. And even here the focus on wellbeing with empirical support varies significantly.

Conceptual links between wellbeing and safety

Most discussions on the importance of wellbeing related to safety emerge from reviews of links between organizational practices and employee wellbeing typically focused on general aspects of employee health and performance. However, expanding the approach to employee health – including aspects of workplace wellbeing and safety, allows inferences to be made about specific relationships (Danna & Griffin, 1999; Grant, Christianson & Price, 2007; Grawitch, Gottschalk & Munz, 2006; Manser, 2009). All advance the construct that employee wellbeing is the most effective mechanism in leading to safety practices with increased safety and overall organizational performance.

For example, in healthcare, a field that produces a high volume of studies and research on teamwork and its impact on the safety of patient care, Manser (2009) argues that the way the staff perceive leaders and teams influences their wellbeing, with a potentially negative impact on their ability to provide safe patient care. Hall *et al.* (2016) arrive to the same conclusion in a review on healthcare staff wellbeing, burnout, and patient safety. Most studies reveal that low levels of employee wellbeing and moderate to high levels of burnout are associated with negative safety outcomes, and tend to increase the number of medical errors.

In a broader review, Grawitch *et al.* (2006) show that healthy workplace practices increase employee wellbeing and improve organizational performance. These authors propose a direct and an indirect path to link organizational practices with improvements including employee wellbeing. While health and safety programs are listed among the organizational practices considered, the focus is on physical health initiatives, rather than safety. The authors argue that these initiatives result in organizational support that contributes to wellbeing, reducing levels of stress. Furthermore, employee wellbeing impacts workplace practices, organizational improvements, and successful outcome. They claim that employee wellbeing should not be considered a byproduct of health initiatives, but rather a critical factor in achieving expected organizational outcomes. This argument is discussed next.

Grant *et al.* (2007) expand the discussion, considering the relationships between various aspects of wellbeing, and the temporal aspects of these relationships, supporting the idea that wellbeing acts as the main mechanism linking managerial practices to outcomes, and drawing attention to the multidimensional nature of wellbeing and potential trade-offs. Working with a comprehensive definition of wellbeing that includes physical, psychological, and social aspects, Grant *et al.* argue that safety practices aimed to improve physical health might have the potential to introduce a negative effect on aspects of psychological wellbeing. The authors highlight that when safety practices have an initial negative effect on employee psychological wellbeing, overtime time they can fail to protect physical wellbeing due to lack in safety compliance, and affect social wellbeing due to compromised working relationships. It is apparent that any attempt at integrating health and safety has to take into consideration potential positive and negative synergies between all aspects of wellbeing. Moreover, timing is critical because aspects of psychological wellbeing at work are immediately sensitive to practices carrying effects on wellbeing dimensions.

Empirical evidence linking employee wellbeing and safety

Ideas advanced in theoretical reviews have not received consistent empirical support. Studies presenting empirical investigations on the role of mental health/wellbeing for safety are few and hard to integrate because they investigate different aspects of wellbeing at different levels of analysis. For example, in the safety context, stress is one of the factors that received high attention in some publications. Safety climate and stress are shown as predictors of fatigue-related behavior (Strahan, Watson, & Lennonb, 2008); permanent stress factors can be significant predictors of injuries (Kirschenbaum, Oigenblick, & Goldberg, 2000); and safety appraisals of work (working safely, bending rules, and management safety climate) can affect eustress (stress perceived as a positive challenge), rather than distress (negative stress) (Hansez & Nyssen, 2006).

Studies oriented on general aspects of psychological wellbeing, such as overall mental health, commitment, or satisfaction support the idea that the way organizations approach safety can impact employees' overall wellbeing and these effects might lead to safety outcomes. For example, general mental health (operationalized in terms of general anxiety and depression) can act as a mechanism linking accidents to organizational practices and the physical work environment (Oliver, Cheyne, Tomas, & Cox, 2007). Management commitment to safety is a significant predictor of job satisfaction and affective commitment (Michael, Evans, Jansen, & Haight, 2005).

Hoffman and Mark's study (2006), focused on the relationship between safety climate and indicators of nurses and patients' health, showed a significant relationship between safety climate and nurses' job satisfaction at the unit level. This relationship is strengthened when organizations take a proactive approach to safety. The employees of organizations with a more pro-active approach to OHS management are more committed to their organization and experience greater job satisfaction (Haslam, O'Hara, Kazi, Twumasi, & Haslam, 2016).

The empirical evidence reviewed to this point has mainly addressed general, stable elements of employee wellbeing. However, more specific, dynamic elements of employee wellbeing are necessary to explain the link between safety practices and outcomes.

An interesting insight is provided by Game (2007), who showed that employees who can adapt to cope with boredom at work score higher on work-related wellbeing measures and report higher levels of safety compliance. This implies that, when the mental wellbeing of employees is impaired (people feel bored at work), individuals suffer and organizations do too. Game (2007) also showed that employees who cope better with boredom do it in ways that better align with the organization through positive (finding new ways to complete tasks) rather than negative (reading something unrelated to the job) strategies. Given the importance of designing jobs that reduce boredom and detachment, and that support continuous learning, it is also important to acknowledge that boredom cannot be totally eliminated from contemporary organizations (for example, with highly automated work environments). In these environments the focus should be to provide support to employees, allowing them to adopt coping strategies that promote wellbeing at work in parallel with safety behaviors.

The importance of workplace wellbeing as a mechanism linking organizational safety with policies, practices, and outcomes has been advanced by Nahrgang *et al.* (2011). Their study of 203 samples advances the idea that a mental health impairment process of burnout and a motivational process of engagement can be used to explain how safety specific job demands and resources influence safety outcomes. While the associations reported are encouraging, pointing to the expected links between safety and wellbeing aspects (burnout, engagement), this study did not differentiate between aspects of wellbeing (engagement) and stable aspects such as satisfaction or behaviors such as compliance. Safety outcomes investigated were mostly related to accidents, incidents, and unsafe behavior, leaving aside indicators of general safety performance, organizational improvements, and employee overall wellbeing. Although this study provides initial empirical support to theoretical claims, the importance of workplace wellbeing aspects is still underdeveloped.

The overview this chapter gives of research linking safety and employee wellbeing identifies gaps in the current understanding of the role that employee wellbeing plays to attain safety outcomes. From the perspective of this chapter the focus on wellbeing aspects seems to be secondary to physical health and there is scarce literature approaching the two topics together. Theoretical reviews approaching the topic, directly or indirectly, converge on the idea that the focus on workplace wellbeing can advance the understanding of mechanisms and work characteristics in safety critical contexts and safety practices which can improve outcomes for individuals and organizations. Empirical support for these assumptions remains unclear because, as stated above, different aspects of wellbeing that have been investigated in different studies challenge integration of one construct. Therefore, empirical research needs to be grounded in theoretical development identifying those aspects of workplace wellbeing most relevant to the safety context.

More attention should be given to more dynamic aspects of mental health at work because existent investigations focus on more stable, long-term aspects of employee wellbeing, such as depression, anxiety, satisfaction, and commitment, rather than the more dynamic, state-like aspects (specific feelings or thoughts about particular tasks or situations that occur within a workday) that are more sensitive to changes in parallel with workplace conditions (Sonnentag, 2015). While stable elements, such as satisfaction and commitment, may be expected to change over longer periods of time and in reduced marginal increments, otherwise the ability to gain insights into the most important wellbeing mechanisms is hampered.

As we discussed previously, wellbeing is a broad and complex concept that includes a variety of affects and aspects of psychological and social performance and behaviors (Diener, 2000; Lamers, Westerhof, Bohlmeijer, ten Klooster, &

Keyes, 2011; Warr, 1990). It refers to a global and often stable evaluation of one's life and context specific aspects and also momentary mood and experiences (Diener, 2000). To understand wellbeing in the context of workplace safety, research should focus on wellbeing aspects that are specific to work and that are directly influenced by work-related factors.

To understand how organizations can actively support employee wellbeing and safety it is necessary to shift focus from general to situational wellbeing, although long-term effects on employees' general wellbeing and health can also be assumed. Situational wellbeing is an evaluation of an employee's state at a specific moment in time and can also be an indicator of long-term wellbeing achievement (Sonnentag, 2001). In this chapter, we argue that careful consideration of situational wellbeing elements pertaining to work versus long-term, general individual wellbeing helps to advance understanding of the role wellbeing plays in safety outcomes. In the model we propose, situational work wellbeing, defined in terms of active psychological states (APS), presents the mechanism that influences performance and safety outcomes, as well as long-term individual health and wellbeing.

Proposed integrative framework

In this section we propose a framework that identifies active psychological states as the main mechanisms of work-related wellbeing that explain the effects of individual and contextual factor on employee safety and overall wellbeing and health (Figure 5.1). We describe the main elements of this framework together with existing literature supporting inclusions. We identify future research directions to facilitate understanding the role of work-related wellbeing in relation to organizational safety.

Figure 5.1 Overview of antecedents and consequences related to active psychological states (APS) at work.

Source: Authors.

Active psychological states: a dynamic resource for safety and general health and wellbeing

"Active psychological states" (APS) represent a complex concept that articulates a fundamental link between health and safety goals. APS represent the ongoing adaptive capability of an individual that is derived from affective engagement, cognitive control, and resource replenishment. APS are dynamic states that are likely to vary each day under the influence of factors related to the individual and his/her work. For individuals, APS are a source of wellbeing and motivate a range of proactive safety behaviors in the workplace. Variation in APS is influenced by organizational practices and resources such as the design of jobs and management behavior.

We use the term "active psychological states" to encompass a variety of concepts that promote performance and learning in the workplace and are central to human centered management (Lepeley, 2017). These states are dynamic psychological resources that are shaped by the organizational context and that translate into long-term outcomes such as health and performance through individual adaptation and innovation (Parker & Griffin, 2011). The common feature of these states is a positive activation of psychological resources through affective engagement, confidence, and energy. An essential underpinning of all these states is that they help to explain the active process through which people develop their capabilities over time (Bandura, 2000).

APS act as psychological resources that contribute to self-initiated behaviors and wellbeing. As an example of APS, Spreitzer *et al.* (2005) proposed that thriving at work is achieved through a combination of affective experiences such as feeling energized and alive, and cognitive experiences such as continually learning and improving learning.

Below, we will consider the affective and cognitive elements that constitute APS. We also introduce the notion of replenishment as a necessary element of APS based on the extensive literature on recovery from work and its impact on wellbeing.

Affective states: They play an important role in the motivation of proactive behavior and innovation at work (Parker, Bindl, & Strauss, 2010). In particular, activated positive affect, which entails feelings of energy and enthusiasm (Watson, 1988), is considered a key driver of innovation. The practical and theoretical implications of affect for wellbeing as well as safety are well supported, with all definitions of general wellbeing and mental health including hedonic elements (e.g. Diener, 2000; Lamers *et al.*, 2011; Ryan & Deci, 2001) and evidence that frequent experience of momentary positive affect translates into long-term feelings of happiness and life satisfaction that consolidate individual wellbeing.

There is growing evidence that the experience of momentary positive affect leads to success in different aspects of our work and non-work life. For example, Lyubomirsky, King, and Diener (2005) showed that positive affect is associated with a number of desirable characteristics, some of which are particularly relevant to health and wellbeing (such as healthy behaviors, sociability and activity, positive construal of self, prosocial behavior) or to safety, especially proactive participation in safety (such as more creative and more efficient problem solving). Moreover, their work supports the idea that the experience of positive emotions is an antecedent for working more productively, having more satisfying relationships with colleagues, and for superior mental and physical health (Lyubomirsky *et al.*, 2005).

Although the link between positive affect and long-term wellbeing is straightforward, safety outcomes can also be impacted by feelings of activated positive affect experienced at work. This effect is expected to manifest through the active goal involvement that is promoted by positive affect and is beneficial to a range of performance behaviors (Lyubormisky *et al.*, 2005), including safety. Furthermore, concepts closely related to positive emotions, such as satisfaction or engagement, have been shown to predict important safety outcomes, both in terms of behavior and accidents/incidents rates (Nahrgang *et al.*, 2011).

Cognitive states: the cognitive factors associated with APS involve self-efficacy (Yeo & Neal, 2006), perceptions of control (Bakker & Demerouti, 2007), and positive beliefs about learning and change (Parker & Sprigg, 1999) that have been consistently linked to performance and wellbeing (Parker, 2014).

In general, less is known about the role of these active states for safety outcomes (Christian, Bradley, Wallace, & Burke, 2009), although studies have begun to explore this link more directly. For example, in their study using a sample of 239 commercial pilots, Chen and Chen (2014) found direct, positive links between pilots' self-efficacy and their safety behaviors, both in terms of compliance and safety participation. While the authors acknowledge the fact that high self-efficacy might represent a double-edged sword in relation to safety due to increased tendencies to take shortcuts, the effects they reported in this sample are positive. However, this relationship needs to be more carefully considered in other industries, as the aviation industry employs sophisticated solutions for continuous monitoring that might automatically inhibit taking shortcuts.

In a similar way, Fugas, Silva, and Meliá (2012) examined the role of perceived behavioral control over safety and showed that it represents one of the mechanisms that translate the effects of safety climate onto safety compliance behaviors. In a different sample, perceived behavioral control emerged as the variable that best differentiated the groups that consistently behaved in a safer manner (Fugas, Silva, & Meliá, 2013).

Another important insight into the role of cognitive states for safety is provided by research on psychological empowerment. Empowerment is defined as a set of cognitions related to the meaning of work, self-efficacy, self-determination, and impact, shaped by the work environment (Spreitzer, 1995). A comprehensive review (Clarke, 2013) showed that relations characterized by empowerment and participation can act as a support for turning employees' safety intentions into safe behavior. Similarly, Armstrong and Laschinger (2006) provided evidence that leader nurses have the ability to improve the level of patient safety in their organizations by creating an empowering professional practice environment for staff nurses.

Overall, existing evidence supports the idea that active cognitive states that have been traditionally associated with individual wellbeing could also promote safety, not only in terms of safety behaviors of employees but also broader organizational safety outcomes.

Replenishment: We argue that replenishment of resources or recovery is a necessary condition for active engagement. Recovery is "restoration of impaired mood and action prerequisites" and is achieved through detachment, relaxation, mastery, and control (Sonnentag & Fritz, 2007). A need for recovery is a self-regulatory process involving the desire to be relieved from demands in order to restore resources (Sonnentag & Zijlstra, 2006) related to both cognitive and affective states (de Jonge, Dormann, Dollard, Winefield, & Winefield, 2003).

Most research has focused on detachment from work where an individual has a sense of being away from the work situation (Etzion, Eden, & Lapidot, 1998; Sonnentag & Fritz, 2015). This evidence supports the critical role of recovery for employee wellbeing as well as performance (Fritz & Sonnentag, 2006; Sonnentag & Fritz, 2015; Sonnentag & Zijlstra, 2006). But work activities themselves can also be restorative and contribute to recovery, depending on how work interactions generate personal resources (Lilius, 2012).

At first sight, the link between recovery and safety outcomes appears to have received less attention. But if research on fatigue (a concept closely related to the need for recovery) is taken into account, there is strong support for recovery as one of the main contributing factors to accidents, injuries and deaths in a wide variety of settings (Williamson, Lombardi, Folkard, Stutts, Courtney, & Connor, 2011). However, the effects of specific recovery strategies in the context of safety behaviors and outcomes are considerably less understood. This is especially true for those recovery strategies that can be used during work (e.g. restorative work activities) that are extremely relevant for safety critical environments where employees work in roster systems that keep them in a work environment for extended periods of time.

Overall, we argue that replenishment of resources is essential for an active involvement with work that will support not only individual wellbeing in the long term, but also better safety and performance outcomes for the organization.

Health and safety outcomes

In the previous section we underlined critical links between the main elements of APS and outcomes in terms of individual wellbeing and organizational safety. Here we would also like to make further distinctions between health and wellbeing outcomes in the short term and in the longer term.

In the relatively shorter time frame, the experience of APS at work will be reflected in fluctuations in workplace wellbeing and safety proactivity. Over extended periods of time, these fluctuations are expected to accumulate into more stable effects on the overall mental health and wellbeing of employees and their performance capability. The model proposed here focuses primarily on enhancing the understanding of effects for employees' proactive safety behavior and individual wellbeing.

Proactive safety behaviors: Many studies support the idea that employees' active involvement in safety goes beyond simply complying with rules and procedures (Clarke, 2006; Flin, Mearns, O'Connor, & Bryden, 2000). Proactive safety behaviors include activities such as suggesting new ideas, helping co-workers with safety, and anticipating safety problems (Curcuruto & Griffin, 2017) that contribute to the overall safety of a group or organization (Griffin & Neal, 2000). Proactive safety behavior is increasingly recognized as an essential requirement in safety critical environments as it has been shown to influence group safety outcomes over time (Neal & Griffin, 2006). Like other forms of proactivity, we propose that safety proactivity is self-initiated, anticipatory, and change-oriented (Grant & Ashford, 2008; Parker & Collins, 2010).

General wellbeing: This is the positive experience of both satisfaction and meaning in one's life (Ryan & Deci, 2001). It is a desirable state of experiencing positive emotions, purpose, and fulfillment that is increasingly valued by individuals, companies, and societies (Sonnentag, 2015). Recent research argues that we need to adopt a temporal perspective in order to better understand the experience and outcomes of wellbeing (Sonnentag, 2015). The main reason is that wellbeing fluctuates within shorter periods (e.g. days) as well as longer periods of time (e.g. months and years) and that these fluctuations are influenced less by individual characteristics and more by what people experience in their life and by their behaviors.

The proposed model incorporates this temporal perspective by considering both short-term and long-term fluctuations of wellbeing. The short-term perspective is represented by the focus on APS as dynamic wellbeing states that can vary under the immediate influence of different factors in the work environment and in the individual. However, over reasonable periods of time (e.g. months and years), these experiences are expected to accumulate into longer-term effects on the general levels of health and wellbeing of individuals.

Considering different time frames is particularly important in the context of safety critical industries where different roster designs can influence the amount of time employees spend at work as well as their patterns of recovery at work and outside work. There are concerns that wellbeing might deteriorate over longer schedules associated with remote working but a better understanding is needed about the factors that influence employee wellbeing fluctuations and how these accumulate over longer periods of time to determine changes in the levels of general wellbeing.

Contextual influences of APS

As mentioned in previous sections, APS are conceptualized here as work-related wellbeing aspects that can fluctuate within a person within relatively shorter periods of time (e.g. within the same day, day to day, or week to week). Literature highlights that these fluctuations can be systematically linked with experiences and events that employees encounter while at work or during non-work hours (Sonnentag, 2015). Therefore, the proposed framework identifies work context and individual factors as the main sources of fluctuations in APS.

Work design: The immediate requirements of the work role create demands and generate resources for employees that have a direct impact on APS and on safety and wellbeing outcomes. Job demands such as physical hazards, time pressure, task complexity, and resources like autonomy, support, or the psychological safety climate are known to influence both safety (Nahrgang *et al.*, 2011) and wellbeing (Bakker & Demerouti, 2007). Therefore, we expect these effects on safety behavior and overall wellbeing to manifest through more immediate fluctuations in employees' APS at work.

In safety critical industries, the use of extended roster systems raises questions about how individuals manage daily recovery to maintain attention and energy over long periods of time.

Organizational culture: Interpersonal factors play an important role for dynamic wellbeing (Sonnentag, 2015) as well as safety-related outcomes (Christian *et al.*, 2009). Research on wellbeing has specifically looked at the role of positive features of the social environment (such as social support) and leadership, which is similar to the increased consideration given to safety culture and leadership for understanding safety-related outcomes (Clarke, 2006; Clarke, 2013).

The role of organizational climate has been one of the most investigated aspects in relation to safety performance or outcomes (Clarke, 2006; Nahrgang *et al.*, 2011). There is increasing evidence on the effects of interpersonal factors on fluctuations of APS, indicating that more positive and supportive climates are able to boost levels of APS during work (Sonnentag, 2015).

In a similar way, leadership and supervision have a strong impact on effectiveness, wellbeing, and safety (Day, Griffin & Louw, 2014; Griffin & Talati, 2014). In particular, the role of team leaders or direct supervisors appears to be most influential as they are in a position that allows them to translate values and goals set by senior management and to provide direct guidance to team members. But different leader behaviors can support different outcomes. For example, inspiring behaviors (e.g. presenting a positive vision of safety to employees) are particularly helpful in facilitating proactive participation is safety. When leaders rely on monitoring behaviors, they will typically facilitate compliance, but when they combine monitoring with behaviors that create a learning supportive environment (e.g. encouraging communication about mistakes) they have the potential to encourage more proactive participation in safety alongside compliance (Griffin &

Hu, 2013). Building on the existing evidence about drivers of participation and compliance, it is expected that facilitating APS during work is one of the mechanisms by which leader behaviors generate these effects.

Individual differences

Evidence indicates that the effects of individual differences might be expected mostly at the level of outcomes in our framework. For example, personal characteristics like safety knowledge, experience, and skills play a key role for safety-related behavior (Griffin & Neal, 2002). In a similar way, stable individual differences will be reflected mostly in longer-term changes in overall wellbeing levels (Sonnentag, 2015). However, evidence is accumulating also for the impact of personal resources (such as abilities to manage emotions and coping) on daily fluctuations of work-related wellbeing (Weigl, Hornung, Parker, Petru, Glaser, & Angerer, 2010).

Another important role for experiencing APS is played by personal factors situated at the interface between work and non-work life (Sonnentag, 2015). Among these, recovery activities after work (e.g. physical exercise) and the conflict between work and family life have received particular attention in the context of wellbeing.

Taken together, these findings support the idea that, in order to facilitate wellbeing at work, individual interventions might be targeted at improving personal resources while also facilitating a work environment that minimizes negative interference with family or social life. These interventions have the potential to increase employee resilience over time and contribute to positive outcomes for the individual and the organizations (Lepeley, 2017).

Practical implications

In this chapter, we argue for a more systematic understanding of the interplay between safety and wellbeing, particularly relevant to safety critical work contexts where individuals are likely to face more challenging conditions such as remote locations and hazardous work.

The framework we propose for integrating wellbeing and proactive safety extends to current approaches, which traditionally focus on the negative elements of mental health and on the compliant aspects of safety management. Despite the importance of these initiatives, a better understanding of positive mental health in terms of wellbeing and of safety in terms of proactivity has a number of benefits, some of which will be briefly highlighted in this section.

First, work environments are changing at faster rates due to technological advancement and demographic changes, among other pressures. As a result, having a more adaptive, agile, and thriving workforce becomes crucial in obtaining a competitive advantage for all organizations, industries, sectors, and nations worldwide (Griffin, Neal & Parker, 2007; Lepeley, 2017). Therefore, a systematic approach to facilitate individual health and wellbeing at work in a way that supports important organizational outcomes such as safety is no longer an option but an imperative.

Second, this refocus comes in alignment with wider policy frameworks proposed. For example, *Health 2020*, the new European policy framework for health and wellbeing (WHO, 2013), supports the idea that good health is a vital ingredient for economic recovery and social development, drawing obvious links between health and broader organizational and societal outcomes. The main themes among the four priority areas are empowerment of individuals, increased individual and social capabilities, and resilience. We believe that the framework we provided here is in alignment with these policy priorities and highlights how these outcomes can be supported at the organizational level. Therefore, it can serve as a framework for guiding the design and development of policies and intervention programs in organizations that can contribute to social development and economic growth.

By actively supporting the experience of positive affective engagement, cognitive controls, and replenishment while at work, the organizations can take an active part in supporting the development of individual and psychosocial resources in their employees that directly contribute to supportive, resilient, and healthy environments and communities.

Last but not least, through our focus on learning and development supported by APS, we believe that our framework provides an opportunity to contribute to more sustainable ways of functioning and more sustainable organizations. Sustainability implies learning processes at different levels, from individual to societal, and involves a strong motivation to act in sustainable ways (Hansmann, 2010). By highlighting those factors that contribute to individual learning and motivation, the framework proposed here has the potential to contribute to increased organizational sustainability.

But how can organizations practically achieve these outcomes? While the framework we proposed here is a broad one, its development is based on the core idea that there is theoretical support for a **strategic integration of human resources polices and safety policies** that could generate and sustain competitive advantage for contemporary organizations. Moreover, by focusing on the APS of employees that constitute the basis for an overall active involvement in work and life, policies and interventions can simultaneously contribute to the achievement of several individual, organizational, and societal outcomes. Therefore, organizations will need to reassess and align systems and practices in order to promote active psychological states (affect, positive thoughts, and recovery) in their employees. Our framework points to the different levers by which this can be achieved, from building individual resources to more purposefully balancing leadership behaviors and organizational culture. This is even more critical as the relevance of health and safety is transcending more and more the traditional high risk industry, becoming relevant not only for the large resource sector, but also for small scale mining (Smith, Ali, Bofinger, & Collins, 2016), micro-firms (Boustras, Hadjimanolis, Economides, Yiannaki, & Nicolaides, 2015), or nanotechnology (Gendre, Blackburn, Brighton, Rodriguez, & Abhyankar, 2015), just to give a few examples.

Another important aspect that is highlighted in our framework is the fact that broader organizational factors can simultaneously contribute to individual wellbeing and organizational safety. Health and safety are not the sole responsibility of the Health and Safety Department, or of the Health and Safety professionals. It is intertwined with all aspects of organizational functioning as all employees have a personal responsibility for safety, while all organizational systems and practices have direct or indirect implications for safety. Therefore, we argue that **an organizational climate and balanced leadership behaviors that promote the active involvement and empowerment of all employees** in all aspects of work will benefit not only health and safety outcomes, but also overall productivity, competitiveness and innovation.

The proposed framework is built around the idea that the everyday work experiences and environment are contributing to wellbeing variations that can accumulate in time. Therefore, the focus shifts from the individual factors that contribute to overall wellbeing levels to the organization and the nature of work itself. To actively support organizations in creating healthier and safer environments for employees, it is critical to support a better understanding of the way the work itself and what happens at work is contributing to workplace wellbeing. Therefore, a more careful consideration of work experiences through work design and redesign is imperative. To actively support APS at work, organizations have to promote a healthy balance between the work demands that are placed upon employees and the resources they afford employees, so that employees are challenged, but at the same time offered the necessary tools to respond adaptively and to actively engage in their work for the long-term benefit of the individual and the organization.

In conclusion, contemporary social, financial, and environmental pressures are creating the need for innovative approaches to create human centered organizations. Organizational Health and Safety policies, integrated and aligned with organizational strategic goals supporting employees' learning and wellbeing at work, expand necessary agility to adapt to changes and induce change and innovation that foster progress in all kinds of organizations.

References

Armstrong, K.J., & Laschinger, H. (2006). Structural empowerment, Magnet hospital characteristics, and patient safety culture: making the link. *Journal of Nursing Care Quality*, *21*(2), 124–132.

Bakker, A.B., & Demerouti, E. (2007). The job demands-resources model: State of the art. *Journal of managerial psychology, 22*(3), 309–328.

Bandura, A. (2000). Exercise of human agency through collective efficacy. *Current directions in psychological science, 9*(3), 75–78.

Boustras, G., Hadjimanolis, A., Economides, A., Yiannaki, A., & Nicolaides, L. (2015). Management of health and safety in micro-firms in Cyprus: Results from a Nationwide Survey. *Safety science, 79*, 305–313.

Caulfield, N., Chang, D., Dollard, M.F., & Elshaug, C. (2004). A Review of Occupational Stress Interventions in Australia. *International Journal of Stress Management, 11*(2), 149.

Chen, C.F., & Chen, S.C. (2014). Measuring the effects of Safety Management System practices, morality leadership and self-efficacy on pilots' safety behaviors: Safety motivation as a mediator. *Safety science, 62*, 376–385.

Christian, M.S., Bradley, J.C., Wallace, J.C., & Burke, M.J. (2009). Workplace safety: A meta-analysis of the roles of person and situation factors. *Journal of Applied Psychology, 94*(5), 1103–1127.

Clarke, S. (2006). The relationship between safety climate and safety performance: a meta-analytic review. *Journal of occupational health psychology, 11*(4), 315.

Clarke, S. (2013). Safety leadership: A meta-analytic review of transformational and transactional leadership styles as antecedents of safety behaviours. *Journal of Occupational and Organizational Psychology, 86*(1), 22–49.

Curcuruto, M., & Griffin, M.A. (2017). Safety proactivity in organizations: The initiative to improve individual, team and organizational safety. In S.K. Parker & U.K. Bindl (Eds.), *Proactivity at work. Making things happen in organizations* (pp. 105–137). London, UK: Routledge.

Danna, K., & Griffin, R.W. (1999). Health and well-being in the workplace: A review and synthesis of the literature. *Journal of management, 25*(3), 357–384.

Day, D.V., Griffin, M.A., & Louw, K.R. (2014). The climate and culture of leadership in Organizations. In B. Schneider & K. M. Barbera (Eds.), *The Oxford Handbook of Organizational Climate and Culture* (pp. 101–117). Oxford: Oxford University Press.

de Jonge, J., Dormann, C., Dollard, M.F., Winefield, H.R., & Winefield, H.R. (2003). The DISC model: Demand-induced strain compensation mechanisms in job stress. In *Occupational stress in the service professions* (pp. 43–74). London: Taylor & Francis.

Diener, E. (2000). Subjective well-being: The science of happiness and a proposal for a national index. *American psychologist, 55*(1), 34.

Etzion, D., Eden, D., & Lapidot, Y. (1998). Relief from job stressors and burnout: reserve service as a respite. *Journal of Applied Psychology, 83*(4), 577.

Flin, R., Mearns, K., O'Connor, P., & Bryden, R. (2000). Measuring safety climate: identifying the common features. *Safety science, 34*(1–3), 177–192.

Fritz, C., & Sonnentag, S. (2006). Recovery, well-being, and performance-related outcomes: the role of workload and vacation experiences. *Journal of Applied Psychology, 91*(4), 936.

Fugas, C.S., Silva, S.A., & Meliá, J.L. (2012). Another look at safety climate and safety behavior: Deepening the cognitive and social mediator mechanisms. *Accident Analysis & Prevention, 45*, 468–477.

Fugas, C.S., Silva, S.A., & Meliá, J.L. (2013). Profiling safety behaviors: Exploration of the sociocognitive variables that best discriminate between different behavioral patterns. *Risk analysis, 33*(5), 838–850.

Game, A.M. (2007). Workplace boredom coping: Health, safety, and HR implications. *Personnel Review, 36*(5), 701–721.

Gendre, L., Blackburn, K., Brighton, J., Rodriguez, V.M., & Abhyankar, H. (2015). Nanomaterials Life Cycle Analysis: Health and safety practices, standards and Regulations – past, present and future perspective. *International Research Journal of Pure and Applied Chemistry, 5*(3), 208.

Grant, A.M., & Ashford, S. (2008). The dynamics of proactivity at work. *Research in Organizational Behavior, 28*, 3–34.

Grant, A.M., Christianson, M.K., & Price, R.H. (2007). Happiness, health, or relationships? Managerial practices and employee well-being tradeoffs. *The Academy of Management Perspectives, 21*(3), 51–63.

Grawitch, M.J., Gottschalk, M., & Munz, D.C. (2006). The path to a healthy workplace: A critical review linking healthy workplace practices, employee well-being, and organizational improvements. *Consulting Psychology Journal: Practice and Research, 58*(3), 129.

Griffin, M.A., & Hu, X. (2013). How leaders differentially motivate safety compliance and safety participation: The role of monitoring, inspiring, and learning. *Safety Science, 60*, 196–202.

Griffin, M.A., & Neal, A. (2000). Perceptions of safety at work: A framework for linking safety climate to safety performance, knowledge, and motivation. *Journal of occupational health psychology, 5*(3), 347–358.

Griffin, M.A., & Talati, Z. (2014). Safety leadership. In D. Day (Ed.), *The Oxford handbook of leadership and organizations* (pp. 638–656). New York, NY: Oxford University Press.

Griffin, M.A., Neal, A., & Parker, S.K. (2007). A new model of work role performance: Positive behavior in uncertain and interdependent contexts. *Academy of management journal, 50*(2), 327–347.

Hall, L.H., Johnson, J., Watt, I., Tsipa, A., & O'Connor, D.B. (2016). Healthcare staff wellbeing, burnout, and patient safety: A systematic review. *PloS one, 11*(7), e0159015.

Hansez, I., & Nyssen, A. S. (2006). Impact of work variables and safety appraisal on well-being at work. In *Proceedings of the 16th World Congress of Ergonomics*. Elsevier.

Hansmann, R. (2010). "Sustainability learning": An introduction to the concept and its motivational aspects. *Sustainability, 2*(9), 2873–2897.

Harter, J.K., Schmidt, F.L., & Hayes, T.L. (2002). Business-unit-level relationship between employee satisfaction, employee engagement, and business outcomes: a meta-analysis. *Journal of applied psychology, 87*(2), 268.

Haslam, C., O'Hara, J., Kazi, A., Twumasi, R., & Haslam, R. (2016). Proactive occupational safety and health management: Promoting good health and good business. *Safety science, 81*, 99–108.

Kirschenbaum, A., Oigenblick, L., & Goldberg, A. I. (2000). Well being, work environment and work accidents. *Social Science & Medicine, 50*(5), 631–639.

Kompier, M.A., Cooper, C.L., & Geurts, S.A. (2000). A multiple case study approach to work stress prevention in Europe. *European Journal of Work and Organizational Psychology, 9*, 371–400.

Lamers, S., Westerhof, G.J., Bohlmeijer, E.T., ten Klooster, P.M., & Keyes, C.L. (2011). Evaluating the psychometric properties of the mental health continuum-short form (MHC_SF). *Journal of clinical psychology, 67*(1), 99–110.

Lepeley, M.T. (2017). *Human Centered Management. The Five Pillars of Quality Organizations and Global Sustainability*. Saltaire, UK: Greenleaf.

Lilius, J. M. (2012). Recovery at work: Understanding the restorative side of "depleting" client interactions. *Academy of Management Review, 37*(4), 569–588.

Lyubomirsky, S., King, L., & Diener, E. (2005). The benefits of frequent positive affect: does happiness lead to success? *Psychological bulletin,131*(6), 803–855.

Manser, T. (2009). Teamwork and patient safety in dynamic domains of healthcare: A review of the literature. *Acta Anaesthesiologica Scandinavica, 53*(2), 143–151.

Michael, J.H., Evans, D.D., Jansen, K.J., & Haight, J.M. (2005). Management commitment to safety as organizational support: Relationships with non-safety outcomes in wood manufacturing employees. *Journal of Safety Research, 36*(2), 171–179.

Nahrgang, J.D., Morgeson, F.P., & Hofmann, D.A. (2011). Safety at work: A meta-analytic investigation of the link between job demands, job resources, burnout, engagement, and safety outcomes. *Journal of Applied Psychology, 96*(1), 71–94.

Neal, A., & Griffin, M. A. (2006). A study of the lagged relationships among safety climate, safety motivation, safety behavior, and accidents at the individual and group levels. *Journal of Applied Psychology, 91*(4), 946–953.

Oliver, A., Cheyne, A., Tomas, J.M., & Cox, S. (2002). The effects of organizational and individual factors on occupational accidents. *Journal of Occupational and Organizational psychology, 75*(4), 473–488.

Parker, S.K. (2014). Beyond motivation: Job and work design for development, health, ambidexterity, and more. *Annual Review of Psychology, 65*(1), 661–691.

Parker, S.K., Bindl, U.K., & Strauss, K. (2010). Making things happen: A model of proactive motivation. *Journal of Management, 36*(4), 827- 856.

Parker, S.K., & Collins, C.G. (2010). Taking stock: Integrating and differentiating multiple proactive behaviors. *Journal of Management, 36*(5), 633–662.

Parker, S.K., & Griffin, M.A. (2011). Understanding active psychological states: Embedding engagement in a wider nomological net and closer attention to performance. *European Journal of Work and Organizational Psychology, 20*(1), 60–67.

Parker, S.K., & Sprigg, C.A. (1999). Minimizing strain and maximizing learning: the role of job demands, job control, and proactive personality. *Journal of Applied Psychology, 84*(6), 925–939.

Ryan, R.M., & Deci, E.L. (2001). To be happy or to be self-fulfilled: A review of research on hedonic and eudaimonic well-being. *Annual Review of Psychology, 52*, 141–166.

Smith, N.M., Ali, S., Bofinger, C., & Collins, N. (2016). Human health and safety in artisanal and small-scale mining: an integrated approach to risk mitigation. *Journal of Cleaner Production, 129*, 43–52.

Sonnentag, S. (2001). Work, recovery activities, and individual well-being: A diary study. *Journal of occupational health psychology, 6*(3), 196.

Sonnentag, S. (2015). Dynamics of well-being. *Annual Review of Organizational Psychology and Organizational Behavior, 2*(1), 261–293.

Sonnentag, S., & Fritz, C. (2007). The Recovery Experience Questionnaire: development and validation of a measure for assessing recuperation and unwinding from work. *Journal of Occupational Health Psychology, 12*(3), 204–221.

Sonnentag, S., & Fritz, C. (2015). Recovery from job stress: The stressor-detachment model as an integrative framework. *Journal of Organizational Behavior, 36*(S1), S72-S103.

Sonnentag, S., & Zijlstra, F.R. (2006). Job characteristics and off-job activities as predictors of need for recovery, well-being, and fatigue. *Journal of Applied Psychology, 91*(2), 330.

Spreitzer, G. M. (1995). Psychological empowerment in the workplace: Dimensions, measurement, and validation. *Academy of Management Journal, 38*(5), 1442–1465.

Spreitzer, G., Sutcliffe, K., Dutton, J., Sonenshein, S., & Grant, A.M. (2005). A socially embedded model of thriving at work. *Organization Science, 16*(5), 537–549.

Strahan, C., Watson, B., & Lennonb, A. (2008). Can organisational safety climate and occupational stress predict work-related driver fatigue? *Transportation research part F: traffic psychology and behaviour, 11*(6), 418–426.

Warr, P. (1990). The measurement of well-being and other aspects of mental health. *Journal of Occupational Psychology, 63*(3), 193–210.

Watson, D. (1988). Intraindividual and interindividual analyses of positive and negative affect: Their relation to health complaints, perceived stress, and daily activities. *Journal of personality and social psychology*, *54*(6), 1020.

Weigl, M., Hornung, S., Parker, S.K., Petru, R., Glaser, J., & Angerer, P. (2010). Work engagement accumulation of task, social, personal resources: A three-wave structural equation model. *Journal of Vocational Behavior*, *77*(1), 140–153.

Williamson, A., Lombardi, D.A., Folkard, S., Stutts, J., Courtney, T.K., & Connor, J.L. (2011). The link between fatigue and safety. *Accident Analysis & Prevention*, *43*(2), 498–515.

World Health Organization WHO. (2013). *Health 2020. A European policy framework and strategy for the 21st century*. www.euro.who.int/en/health-topics/health-policy/health-2020-the-european-policy-for-health-and-well-being/about-health-2020/priority-areas

Yeo, G. B., & Neal, A. (2006). An examination of the dynamic relationship between self-efficacy and performance across levels of analysis and levels of specificity. *Journal of Applied Psychology, 91*(5), 1088–1101.

6 Wellbeing@work

Is buffering stress enough?

Peter Essens and Maria-Teresa Lepeley

Introduction

A recent study on stress among hospital employees in emergency rooms (ER) conducted in 19 hospitals in the Netherlands showed that, regardless of their positions and level of responsibility as doctors or nurses, employees had substantial levels of psychosocial overloads with 47 percent of them scoring high on burnout indicators (de Wijn & van der Doef, 2017). Another study on ER nurses showed that on average 26 percent of ER nurses suffer high level of burnout (Adriaenssens *et al.*, 2014).

We present these examples to express the sense of urgency that stress and burnout has in the workplace because high level of burnout is predictive of longer-term illness (Borrits *et al.*, 2010).

Although working in emergency rooms may present extreme conditions, workers in other sectors also report similarly high levels of burnout that are seldom accounted for. A nationwide study of employee burnout including all sectors of the workforce in the Netherlands reported high levels of burnout complaints. Twenty percent of employees in education and 15 percent in health care reported comparatively high scores – over 3.2 on a 7-point scale (NEA, 2016).

Burnout indicators relate to states of feeling emotionally exhausted several times a month or more often. Feelings include loss of concern, psychological withdrawal from relationships, negative and cynical feelings and attitudes, lack of enthusiasm in personal accomplishment, and failure to achieve goals (Maslach, Schaufeli, & Leiter, 2008).

Dealing with stress and burnout

Studies on stress and burnout suggest a rising trend (Johnson *et al.*, 2018; Shanafelt *et al.*, 2015; Smulders *et al.*, 2013). In practice, burnout complaints in the Netherlands have increased from 10 percent to 13 percent between 1997 and 2012 (Smulders *et al.*, 2013). A study comparing level of burnout among physicians in the US between 2011 and 2014 showed a 9 percent rise (Shanafelt *et al.*, 2015). A UK study of 53 percent of health care workers reports that stress is the most common cause of long-term absenteeism and 47 percent reports it as the second cause of short-term absenteeism (CIPD, 2016), with highest levels in three sectors: health, public administration, and education (Black & Frost, 2011).

A longitudinal study of evolution in work-related exhaustion in 13 countries in the European Union and the US showed that, in all but two countries, the levels of burnout complaints remained constant *on average* between 1997 and 2005. But complaints vary across groups and between skilled and semi-skilled groups (Steiber & Pichler, 2015), workers that begin temporary jobs (Smulders *et al.*, 2016), and workers in education and health sector compared with the general working population (Shanafelt *et al.*, 2015; NEA, 2016).

Today stress is a serious issue in the workplace in all sectors because of the consequence and negative impact on the wellbeing and personal lives of workers, and the performance and productivity of organizations and the workforce.

It is common to hear that attention on psychosocial stress grew due to deep transformation from an industrial society into a service economy, and has lately expanded by the effects of globalization or the economic crisis (EU-OSHA, 2014; Mucci *et al.*, 2016). But the most negative trends appear to be related to work intensity and job insecurity, flexible contracts. and reduction of workers' autonomy to make decisions (Gallie *et al.*, 2014).

A growing concern for organizations and management is the costs associated with work-related stress and burnout, and work-related illness and absenteeism, which affect the working culture of organizations (Toppinen-Tanner *et al.*, 2005). Besides ethical concerns, in most countries with increasing legal obligations to provide healthy work environments, there are high costs associated with work-related illness and stress: the EU reports between €200 and €300 billion and US $300 billion a year, based on 1979 figures, and estimates have grown since then (EU-OSHA, 2014). These costs do not include human costs, such as loss of quality of life and diminishing level of wellbeing at work and at home. While a standard way of calculating costs for comparison seems to be missing, figures indicate substantial organizational and societal costs of illness related to the workplace.

The World Health Organization describes a healthy workplace one "where pressures on employees are appropriate in relation to their abilities and resources, to the amount of control they have over their work, and support they receive from people who matter for them" (Stavroula, Griffiths, & Cox, 2004). Solutions and interventions to decrease stress and burnout associated risk factors require the attention of managers and executives in organizations, policy makers, and, overall, of the employees, who are mostly impacted. Given the effects of stress and burnout in the labor force and society, in addition to organizational and personal costs, solutions will only be possible with concerted efforts and effective human centered structures and strategies to alleviate recurrent problems (Lepeley, 2017).

But new questions arise. Referring back to the ER case cited in the introduction, it is clear that stressful conditions have existed in the workplace for a longer time and this is confirmed by the large number of studies (e.g. Adriaenssens *et al.*, 2014). This leads us to think that change is difficult, and solutions are challenging. Then what models are feasible to analyze and assess stressful conditions at work to find solutions?

We conducted a literature scan and found that work-related stress and burnout have received increasing interest since 1978. For instance, burnout has been addressed in behavioral and social science and medical literature (PsycINFO, MEDLINE) in over 24,000 publications between 1978 and 2017. We also scanned developments in wellbeing literature (PsycINFO, MEDLINE) and found more than 25,000 publications between 1978 and 2017.

But when we searched stress-burnout combined with wellbeing we found only 400 publications in 40 years, with 375 in the last decade. This shows that, in relative terms, burnout and wellbeing at work have evolved separately and the relationship between them is an emerging concern and an urgent need.

Dealing with job demands and resources available

Recognized theories explaining and predicting job-related work stress and burnout state that it happens when *job demands* are high and *job resources* available to the employee are limited to deal effectively with the demands, resulting in decreased performance. It seems natural that adding resources would increase an employee's energy and motivation to cope with job demands. On this token, the Job Demands-Resources (JD-R) model integrates various models to address relationships between job characteristics and demands, level of energy, resources, and motivation at work (Demerouti *et al.*, 2001; Bakker & Demerouti, 2007; Bakker & Demerouti, 2017). Below there is a description of these factors.

The Job Demands-Resource (JD-R) model

Job demands are aspects of work that require physical, cognitive and emotional effort, including time pressure, work overload, role ambiguity, and conflict. Job resources are aspects that expedite achievement of an employee's work goals induced by energy and personal growth. Job resources are all the aspects related to organizational environment (learning opportunities, responsibility, autonomy, organizational resources), social relations (support, team work), work (diversity, role clarity), and tasks (challenging, competencies). Personal resources are related to self-efficacy, self-esteem, and resilience, which add value and create the feeling of being better prepared and able to handle job demands (Xanthopoulou *et al.*, 2007).

The JD-R model has the capacity to predict negative and positive work outcomes, identifying processes leading to burnout, health impairment, and motivational reactions steering work engagement. Both concepts, burnout and engagement, are considered to be elements of wellbeing.

Engagement is the positive counterpart of burnout, not an opposite per se, but an independent and distinct concept. The inclusion of the engagement concept in the model evolved along the emergence of positive psychology focused on human strengths and psychological capacities (Schaufeli *et al.*, 2009). Positive psychology aims "to build qualities that help individuals and communities to endure and survive and also flourish" (Seligman & Csikszentmihalyi, 2000).

Figure 6.1 shows the structure of the JD-R model with the effects the elements have: higher demands result in higher stress response, and job resources and personal resources buffer the negative effect of job demands, resulting in a lower stress response. The same reasoning applies to other effects shown in Figure 6.1. Some effects run in both directions – for instance job demands may exhaust job resources, and job resources may have limiting effects on job demands. Arrows indicate a positive or strengthening (+) effect or a negative or suppressing (–) effect.

The JD-R model plays a useful role in practical work assessments because it has a strong intuitive appeal, is generic, can adapt to a wide variety of settings where demands and resources play a role, and is easy to apply in practice (Schaufeli, 2017; Bakker & Demerouti, 2017).

Advancing solutions: challenges and hindrances

A new development regarding the positive and negative effects of work conditions on wellbeing is the differentiation between work demands that consume energy but also generate energy, and demands that mainly hinder and frustrate work efforts.

The JD-R model claims that job demands create strain and energy loss and eventually exhaustion when insufficient resources are available. In contrast, some studies show that some job demands may have a positive motivating effect (LePine, LePine & Jackson, 2004; Crawford, Lepine & Rich, 2010). For example, demands such as workload, time pressure, and a high level of responsibility can *challenge* and encourage workers to attain higher goals.

Meanwhile, demands such as role ambiguity, organizational politics, and red tape are appraised as obstacles that *hinder* goal attainment. The point here is that a demand is appraised as a positive challenge when the person trusts that increased

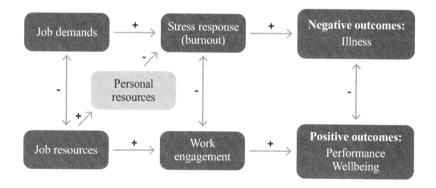

Figure 6.1 The Job Demands-Resources JD-R model.
Source: After Xanthopoulou *et al.* (2007).

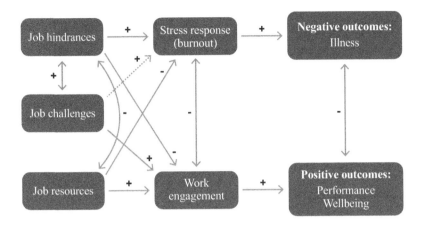

Figure 6.2 Challenge–Hindrance–Stress model.
Source: LePine, LePine & Jackson (2004) and Van Den Broeck *et al.* (2010).

efforts lead to increased performance and higher reward. This process is illustrated in the Challenge–Hindrance–Stress model in Figure 6.2. Arrows indicate a positive (+) or negative / suppressing (–) influence or effect; the dotted line indicates an effect with mixed findings.

Workload is a recurrent theme in work-related assessments in the workplace and is generally assessed as main cause for stress and burnout. Instead, the Challenge-Hindrance concept posits that workload, as a typical work demand, may have positive value and provide opportunities to master work challenges, develop new ways to deal with demands, and may trigger positive processes of creativity and endurance.

While hindrances have potential to develop feelings of exhaustion and loss in work engagement, high work demands, even when appraised as positive and contributing energy, could still consume more energy than job resources contribute. Indeed, some studies have found that high work demands contribute to work engagement as well as to burnout (LePine *et al.*, 2004; Crawford *et al.*, 2010). However, others only found positive effects on work engagement and no direct effect on burnout (Van den Broeck *et al.*, 2010; and confirmed by Essens in unpublished research).

The assumption that not all demands are equal, and that workload can have positive effects, is an important step forward in identifying work conditions that generate strain.

The buffer hypothesis – is buffering enough?

There are several ways resources may reduce the effects of job demands. For instance, supervisors or colleagues may make sense of the demanding work condition and in this way change the perception of the stressor; or by providing more autonomy workers may organize their work differently; or (extra) colleagues may be available for taking over if needed, potentially breaking the causal chain from demands to stress.

The buffer hypothesis is supported in multiple studies on job stress in occupational settings, social support in interpersonal settings, and clinical settings (Bakker & Demerouti, 2007; Cohen & Wills, 1985; Haines, Hurlbert & Zimmer, 1991). The buffer hypothesis is an appealing concept that assumes that investing in resources can become a valuable strategy (Dean & Lin, 1977; van der Doef & Maes, 1998).

Referring back to the ER case cited in the introduction the employees there showed high scores of burnout and at the same time high work engagement driven by emotional commitment and professionalism to care for patients and collegial support even at the costs of exhaustion – a work condition that is potentially risky. Intervention efforts to build individual buffers against these stress conditions may not be the solution to manage ER job demands. More fundamental structural changes may be needed to achieve sustainable outcomes.

It is common to observe strategies and interventions addressing stress and burnout focused on the individual with limited or no attention to the work environment where the workers operates (Semmer, 2006; Pot, Rus & Oeij, 2017). This focus fits popular positive concepts of individual responsibility, resource building, and development of resilience to counter job and life demands. However, the popularity of the buffering concept, complemented with the JD-R model, individual resilience, and mindfulness concept, may lure managers, executives, and policy makers away from responsible structural and strategic interventions and long-term investment where workers are truly at the center of organizations (Lepeley, 2017).

Strengthening individuals to build buffers to handle work demands is a necessary but not a insufficient condition. Changes in work conditions may be needed to address those work demands. Taking action to improve work conditions is a shared responsibility for workers and their organization. In this environment the organization is responsible for providing stimulating work settings, limiting hindrances, and supporting a positive social climate. Workers are responsible for building resources needed to face work challenges and to manage hindrances, such as creativity to innovate, developing leadership skills, acting effectively in social networks, and seeking to increase personal knowledge and skills that contribute to increasing organization performance and competitiveness.

Worker–organization: integral wellbeing

The theories discussed when combined provide a solid basis for promoting wellbeing in the workplace. This framework can be used as a resource for assessment of the wellbeing status in organizations as well as a basis for developing interventions.

Workers' and organizations' critical elements of wellbeing at work are related to:

(i)   providing challenging work
(ii) limiting hindrances
(iii) building job resources
(iv) developing personal resources
(v)   creating sustainable conditions and outcomes.

Wellbeing, in this case, positions the human being at the center of the organization and supported by the organization (Lepeley, 2017). Productivity is not obtained at the cost of worker's wellbeing, but is a mutual benefit transaction between the organization and the worker, with concrete responsibilities, supported with employee empowerment (meaning, competence, self-determination, impact) and matched with structural strengths allowing them active participation and involvement in decision-making (Laschinger & Read, 2017).

Although sustainable conditions and positive outcomes are often an implicit assumption, they are an explicit element in wellbeing assessment at the workplace (Lepeley, 2017). In particular when interventions intend to improve wellbeing at work by improving these critical elements, the effects should be monitored to observe how wellbeing improves overtime (Mäkikangas *et al.*, 2016).

The five elements of wellbeing are embedded in the integration of workers and the organization. Workers are committed to attaining their best performance to promote high organizational outcome. In turn the organization provides workers with a sustainable environment where they find multiple opportunities to grow personally and socially.

While organizations have the responsibility to guard and improve wellbeing of their employees, they may not have control over some conditions. In the societal environment in which organizations operate today, with global pressures, economic stress, and political choices, the operating conditions may be constrained. Organizations, and their sectors, need to assume responsibility to address (and buffer) demands of the external environment and secure agreement and resources to improve conditions and organizational climate. Moreover, in competitive settings collective actions are necessary to secure the wellbeing of all workers.

Given the interdependence between the individual, the group, the organization, the sector, and societies, buffering at one level is not enough. At each system level buffering and changes of conditions when required may be needed. Building the wellbeing of the labor force today implies high and unavoidable shared commitment to start reducing personal, organizational, and societal costs and constraints to advance to higher human standards.

References

Adriaenssens, J., De Gucht, V., and Maes, S. (2014). Determinants and prevalence of burnout in emergency nurses: A systematic review of 25 years of research. *International Journal of Nursing Studies*, 52, 649–661.

Bakker, A., and Demerouti, E. (2007). The Job Demands-Resources (JD-R) model: State of the art. *Journal of Managerial Psychology*, 22 (3), 309–328.

Bakker, A., and Demerouti, E. (2017). Job Demands–Resources Theory: Taking Stock and Looking Forward. *Journal of Occupational Health Psychology,* 22 (3), 273–285.

Black, C., and Frost, D. (2011). Health at work – an independent review of sickness absence. TSO (The Stationery Office). Available at: www.dwp.gov.uk/docs/health-at-work.pdf. Accessed January 2, 2018.

CIPD (2016). Absence management 2016. Annual Survey report. London: Chartered Institute of Personnel and Development.

Cohen, S., and Wills, T. (1985). Stress, Social Support, and the Buffering Hypothesis. *Psychological bulletin,* 98, 310–357.

Crawford, E.R., LePine, J.A., and Rich, B.L. (2010). Linking job demands and resources to employee engagement and burnout: A theoretical extension and meta-analytic test. *Journal of Applied Psychology*, 95 (5), 834-848.

de Wijn, N., and van der Doef, M. (2017). Psychosocial Workload in Emergency Rooms. Report University Leiden. (*Dutch*: Psychosociale Arbeidsbelasting op de SpoedEisende Hulp (SEH). Available at: www.izz.nl/download/5a3cb54fa77f7.pdf. Accessed January 2, 2018.

Dean, A., and Lin, N. (1977). The stress-buffering role of social support. Problems and prospects for systematic investigation. *The Journal Of Nervous And Mental Disease*, 165 (6), 403–417.

Demerouti, E., Bakker, A.B., Nachreiner, F., and Schaufeli, W.B. (2001). The job demands resources model of burnout. *Journal of Applied Psychology*, 86, 499–512.

EU-OSHA (2014). *Calculating the cost of work-related stress and psychosocial risks.* Bilbao: European Agency for Safety and Health at Work.

Gallie, D., Felstead, A., Green, F., and Inanc, H. (2014). The quality of work in Britain over the economic crisis. *International Review of Sociology*, 24 (2), 207–224.

Haines, V.A., Hurlbert, J.S., and Zimmer, C. (1991). Occupational stress, social support, and the buffer hypothesis. *Work and Occupations*, 18, 212–235.

Johnson, J., Hall, L.H., Berzins, K., Baker, J., Melling, K., and Thompson, C. (2017). Mental healthcare staff well-being and burnout: A narrative review of trends, causes, implications, and recommendations for future interventions. *International Journal of Mental Health Nursing*, 27, 20–32.

Laschinger, H.S., and Read, E. (2017). Workplace empowerment and employee health and wellbeing. In Cary L. Cooper, and Michael P. Leiter (Eds.), *The Routledge Companion to Wellbeing at Work*. Abingdon, UK: Routledge.

Lepeley, M.T. (2017). *Human Centered Management. 5 Pillars of Organizational Quality and Global Sustainability*. Abingdon, UK: Routledge.

LePine, J.A., LePine, M.A., and Jackson, C. (2004). Challenge and Hindrance Stress: Relationships With Exhaustion, Motivation to Learn, and Learning Performance. *Journal of Applied Psychology*, 89 (5), 883–891.

Mäkikangas, A. Schaufeli, W., Leskinen, E., Kinnunen, U. Hyvönen, K., and Feldt, T. (2016). Long-Term Development of Employee Well-Being: A Latent Transition Approach. *Journal of Happiness Studies,* 17, 2325–2345.

Maslach, C., Schaufeli, W.B., and Leiter, M.P. (2001). Job Burnout. *Annual Review of Psychology*, 52, 397–422.

Mucci, N., Giorgi, G., Roncaioli, M., Perez, J.F., and Arcangeli, G. (2016). The correlation between stress and economic crisis: a systematic review. *Neuropsychiatric Disease and Treatment*, 12, 983–993.

NEA, 2016. Nationale Enquête Arbeidsomstandigheden 2016 (TNO/CBS). Available at: www.monitorarbeid.tno.nl/cijfers/nea. Accessed January 2, 2018.

Pot, F.D., Rus, D., and Oeij, P.R.A. (2017). Introduction: The Need to Uncover the Field of Workplace Innovation. In P.R.A. Oeij, D. Rus, and F.D. Pot (Eds.), *Workplace Innovation: Theory, research and practice* (pp. 1–8). Berlin: Springer.

Rydstedt, L. Ferrie, J., and Head, J. (2006). Is there support for curvilinear relationships between psychosocial work characteristics and mental well-being? Cross-sectional and long-term data from the Whitehall II study. *Work & Stress*, 20 (1), 6–20.

Toppinen-Tanner, S., Ojajärvi, A., Väänaänen, A., Kalimo, R., and Jäppinen, P. (2005). Burnout as a Predictor of Medically Certified Sick-Leave Absences and Their Diagnosed Causes. *Behavioral Medicine*, 31 (1), 18–32.

Schaufeli, W.B. (2017). Applying the Job Demands-Resources model: A 'how to' guide to measuring and tackling work engagement and burnout. *Organizational Dynamics*, 46, 120–132.

Schaufeli, W.B., and Bakker, A.B. (2004). Job demands, job resources and their relationship with burnout and engagement: A multi-sample study. *Journal of Organizational Behavior*, 25, 293–315.

Schaufeli, W.B., Salanova, M., Gonzalez-Roma V., and Bakker, A.B. (2002). The measurement of engagement and burnout and: A confirmative analytic approach. *Journal of Happiness Studies*, 3, 71–92.

Schaufeli, W.B., Leiter, W.P., and Maslach, C. (2009). Burnout: 35 years of research and practice. *Career Development International*, 14 (3), 204–220.

Seligman, M.E.P., and Csikszentmihalyi, M. (2000). Positive Psychology: An introduction. *American Psychologist*, 1, 5–14.

Semmer, N.K. (2006). Job stress interventions and the organization of work. *Scandinavian Journal of Work, Environment and Health*, 32 (6, special issue), 515–527.

Shanafelt, T.D., Hasan, O., Dyrbye, L.N., Sinsky, C., Satele, D., Sloan, J., and West, C.P. (2015). Changes in burnout and satisfaction with work-life balance in physicians and the general US working population between 2011 and 2014. In *Mayo Clinic Proceedings*, 90 (12), 1600–1613. New York, NY: Elsevier Science.

Smulders, P., Houtman, I., van Rijssen, J. and Mol, M. (2013). Burnout: Trends, international differences, determinants and effects. *Tijdschrift voor Arbeidsvraagstukken,* 29 (3), 258–278.

Stavroula, L., Griffiths, A., and Cox, T. (2004). Work Organization and stress: Systematic problem approaches for employers, managers and trade union representatives. Geneva: World Health Organization.

Steiber, N., and Pichler, F. (2015). Trends in work stress and exhaustion in advanced economies. *Social Indicators Research*, 121, 215–239.

Van den Broeck, A., De Cuyper, N., De Witte, H., and Vansteenkiste, M. (2010). Not all job demands are equal: Differentiating job hindrances and job challenges in the job demands–resources model. *European Journal of Work and Organizational Psychology*, 19 (6), 735–759.

van der Doef, M. and Maes, S. (1998) The job demand-control(-support) model and physical health outcomes: a review of the strain and buffer hypotheses. *Psychology and Health*, 13, 909–936.

Xanthopoulou, D., Bakker, A.B., Demerouti, E., and Schaufeli, W.B. (2007). The Role of Personal Resources in the Job Demands-Resources Model. *International Journal of Stress Management*, 14 (2), 121–141.

7 Psychosocial risk

A European view

Anabela Correia

Introduction

Rapid change in organizations in all sectors, industries, and across the world is the norm today. Disruptions in the workplace are the consequence of increased use of technology and the economic crisis of the mid 2000 decade, which are impacting deeply on work design and management, inducing profound changes in economies and societies. These changes have driven the emergence of "psychosocial risks" in the workplace and social context that have the potential to cause psychosocial, social, and physical harm (EU-OSHA, 2007).

Work-related psychosocial risks linked to workplace problems such as stress, violence, and harassment are recognized as major contemporary challenges for occupational health and safety, and more broadly for public health (EU-OSHA, 2007; Hupke, 2013; Leka *et al.*, 2013).

The European Survey of Enterprises on New and Emerging Risks – ESENER (EU-OSHA, 2016), covering over 50,000 enterprises in 36 countries across Europe, revealed that workplaces are constantly evolving and affecting workers' health and wellbeing. Among the changes most frequently observed are: significant increase in workers over 55, increasing number of telework employees, fast growing cultural diversity, increased participation of workers with low skills in the language spoken at work, and the unprecedented participation of up to five different generations working together in the same organization. Moreover, the continued growth of the service sector, which entails frequent interactions with customers and more frequent interaction with co-workers, has also contributed to increasing the level of work-related stress and other health problems in organizations.

The psychosocial risk factors most frequently cited by EU-OSHA (2016) are related to: interaction with external customers (including pupils and patients) (58 percent), dealing with pressure to meet deadlines (43 percent), and long work schedule and irregular working hours (23 percent).

Most psychosocial risks are reported in organizations in the service sector (education, health, public administration, accommodation) and the volume of reported risks increases in parallel with the organization's size.

The costs associated with increasing numbers of employees facing psychosocial risks is important because the effects on workers' health hinder individual and organizational performance and productivity, which has a negative impact on competitiveness and national income. In the UK, in 2016/2017, work-related stress caused workers to lose 12.5 million working days, with workers absent for an average of 23.8 days (HSE, 2017).

Stress is reported the second most frequent work-related health problem in the European Union, followed by musculoskeletal disorders (EU-OSHA, 2000; European Commission, 2010).

A Pan-European opinion poll (EU-OSHA, 2013b) revealed that 51 percent of workers mention that stress is common in the workplace and 58 percent state that work-related stress is so common because it is not effectively managed in organizations.

Even though the European Survey of Enterprises on New and Emerging Risks (EU-OSHA, 2016) reports that increasing numbers of corporate executives are concerned about stress and psychosocial risks at work, and a high percentage of organizations are not implementing procedures to manage psychosocial risks. Forty-one percent of the employers surveyed perceived that psychosocial risks are more difficult to manage than "traditional" work-related risks and consider that these problems have greater effect due to lack of information, adequate measurement instruments, and specialized knowledge on psychosocial risk management.

In terms of organization size, 72 percent of large-sized businesses of more than 250 workers implement procedures to manage psychosocial risks, compared with 52 percent among small businesses (20 to 49 workers). In general, larger organizations deploy more comprehensive strategies to prevent psychosocial risks, but in small and medium-sized enterprises (SMEs) expertise, resources, and appropriate methods are lacking.

In terms of training to prevent psychosocial risks, such as stress or bullying, 36 percent of the organizations across the EU-28 stated that this kind of training is offered (EU-OSHA, 2016).

Several initiatives are being deployed in Europe to manage psychosocial risks in the workplace. One of them is the "2014–15 Healthy Workplaces Manage Stress campaign," which includes "Managing Stress and Psychosocial Risks at Work" and the "Healthy Workplaces Good Practice Awards" programs.

Besides this other approaches are used to increase awareness about the importance of recognizing situations that cause stress and other work-related psychosocial risks, aiming to improve risk management and to promote healthy work environments.

All the above identifies the concerns that are boosting interest in developing and implementing prevention programs and creating effective policies to prevent and manage psychosocial risks in the workplace and across organizations in Europe to promote preventive procedures that foster healthier work environments and wellbeing at individual, organizational, and national levels.

This chapter presents key issues associated with psychosocial risks in the workplace in the European Union and discusses how to manage psychological risks. A framework aimed to prevent and reduce psychosocial risks at organizational level is describe and considerations concerning future developments are discussed.

Psychosocial risks, causes, and effects

Psychosocial risk, as a field of study, has been in the literature for decades. However, the study of psychosocial risks at work is a recent development. Psychosocial risks are commonly confused with work-related stress, and there is no clarity between psychosocial risk itself and the factors that induce risks. Therefore, it is important to identify characteristics to help managers across organizations to resolve a growing work-related problem.

The psychosocial work environment focuses on three elements: psychosocial factors, psychosocial risk factors, and psychosocial risks.

Psychosocial factors relate to work responsibilities, organizational climate, and interpersonal relationship. When these factors are positive they foster healthy organizations; when they are negative (called "psychosocial hazards" [Gil-Monte, 2012]), they have a high potential to harm workers' health and wellbeing. Psychosocial hazards are aspects of work that can harm workers' health. Hazards can be induced by unrealistic job demands, lack of job clarity, lack of organizational support, and obstructive organizational climate, and can lead to illness, absenteeism, and increasing amount of human error. All of these result in a lower level of productivity and increasing social costs, including, but not limited to, health care, disability, and early retirement (Leka, 2015; EU-OSHA, 2007, Cox & Griffiths, 2005, as cited in Leka & Jain, 2010).

Psychosocial risks are related to social and economic conditions at work with the potential to affect workers' health, inducing stress, burnout, violence, aggression, harassment, and increasing job insecurity. The difference between psychosocial risk factors and psychosocial risks is severity of consequences. For example, inadequate organizational climate, which is considered a psychosocial risk factor, can induce psychosocial risks like harassment, bullying, and stress. Psychosocial risks can lead to psychosocial hazards that harm workers (Jiménez, 2011).

In Europe, psychosocial risks are largely associated with adverse conditions in organizations, inappropriate management, and negative social context at work commonly related to the following circumstances (Leka & Jain, 2010; EU-OSHA, 2013a):

- workload and work pace: overly demanding work, insufficient time to complete tasks
- role control: low participation in decision-making
- role in organization: ambiguity and conflict
- mismatch between work demands and worker's competences
- interpersonal relationships at work: ineffective communication, lack of support from management and co-workers, conflicting behavior
- harassment or bullying at work

- unfair distribution of work, reward, or career development
- mismanaged organizational change processes and employment vulnerability
- work–family conflict.

The sixth European Working Conditions Survey conducted in 2015 added the following indicators of psychosocial risks (Eurofound, 2016):

- emotional demands
- lack of autonomy
- poor social relationships
- poor leadership.

The following is a list of the most common negative consequences on the health of workers as consequence of psychosocial risks (Cox, Griffiths & Rial-González, 2000; Leka & Jain, 2010; EU-OSHA, 2013a):

- Emotional/psychological: irritability/conflicts,   anxiety/anguish,   sleep disorders, depression, isolation, stress and burnout, family problems, fatigue, sadness, suicide
- Cognitive: lack of concentration, memory, or decision-making problems
- Behavioral: consumption of alcohol, tobacco, drugs, and medications
- Physiological: heart diseases (high blood pressure), gastrointestinal problems, back pain and muscle injury and lower immunity.

Emotional reactions are considered psychological, but they affect cognitive reactions with the high potential to cause physiological responses. These symptoms may show imbalances that, while not commonly not considered illnesses, often precede or precipitate diseases.

The impact of psychosocial risks can be more or less severe, depending on individual characteristics and workers' coping styles. Supervisors should be prepared to detect and manage these pre-conditions to avoid consequences of work-related organizational problems such as absenteeism, turnover, increases in accident rate, reduced productivity, and obstacles to the continuous improvement required to attain quality standards. All of these lead to loss of clients, deterioration of work relations, worker disengagement, common errors, work duplication, and sick leave that significantly impacts on health care cost increases (EU-OSHA, 2013a).

Managing psychosocial risks is synonymous with effective management because employee satisfaction and wellbeing contributes to increased productivity and competitiveness in organizations, induces higher rates of return to human capital, and ultimately fosters economic growth and inclusive societies (Lepeley, 2017).

Although the principal mission of organizations is the satisfaction of the needs and demands of external customers, organizations are unable to produce products and services with quality standards unless the needs of the *internal clients* – the employees – are satisfied first by the organization where they work. To a large extent the success of human centered management depends on effective synchronization of customers' needs and strategies that satisfy the needs of the people who work *in* and *for* the organization (Lepeley, 2017). Organizations unable to meet the needs of customers in sync with the needs of the people who produce products and services will be increasingly unfit to become sustainable in the twenty-first century (Lepeley, 2017).

Management of psychosocial risks is a growing concern for the mental health of workers in organizations and in society at large. For this reason psychological risks should not be seen as a legal obligation but needs to be considered also as an ethical issue (Leka *et al.*, 2008). Corporate social responsibility is an important ongoing development in the EU, and therefore latest guidelines recommend that all organizations work extensively in the improvement of working environments as a necessary condition to decrease – and hopefully eliminate – psychosocial risks that limit human capacity and talent, and hinder the performance, productivity, and competitiveness of the labor force. These are some of the reasons that justify the optimal management of psychosocial risks in organizations across sectors and industries in the European Union (Jain *et al.*, 2011).

Management of psychosocial risks at work

The approaches to manage psychosocial risks differ according to their level of analysis: macro, organizational, and individual. Interventions commonly focus on the organization level, but the macro level (national, European, international) of policy interventions is increasingly important in securing prevention and effective management of psychosocial risks at all levels.

At the macro level, the aim of EU policies is to turn policies into effective practice through the provision of instruments that stimulate and support organizations to prevent and manage psychosocial risks effectively.

Psychosocial risk policies include: development of policies and legislation; risk and psychosocial health monitoring; implementation of policy plans to achieve risk reduction; specification of best practice standards at national and stakeholder levels; stakeholder agreements towards a common strategy; dissemination of best practices, principles, and models; and promoting social dialogue on corporate social responsibility (Leka *et al.*, 2010; Leka *et al.*, 2015b).

Mental health and psychosocial risks in the workplace have been an occupational health and safety priority in the EU in the last decades. European Union organizations have a legal obligation to evaluate and manage psychosocial risks within a set of legal guidelines that make organizations liable for guaranteeing that no harm comes to workers by their work, which includes the prevention of psychosocial risks.

A great deal of legislation has been developed to raise awareness among all stakeholders, organizations, social partners, and employees. However, policies are not developed to the same extent in all European countries, a variation that can be explained by different governmental approaches related to the importance each country gives to psychosocial risks (EU-OSHA, 2014a). There are still shortcomings on clarifying what is mandatory and voluntary concerning security to avoid psychosocial risks.

EU legislation needs to be clarified and harmonized to avoid diverging interpretations and for better coordination at institutional level (Leka *et al.*, 2015b). It is also recommended that management of psychosocial risks avoids segmentation and isolated, ineffective, and unprofitable efforts. Unified effort increases coordination at EU institutional level and participation of all stakeholders and non-traditional stakeholders to achieve maximum impact and returns to investment in these policies and programs.

Although traditional stakeholders, namely trade unions, employers, researchers, academics, government agencies, and OSH services, are important in psychosocial risk management, non-traditional stakeholders, including mental health care institutions, customers/clients, business schools and universities, and employment agencies among others, need to participate more to increase impact in the business sector and society (Jain *et al.*, 2011). The higher the involvement of key stakeholders, the more likely that management of psychosocial issues will become of strategic importance for organizations and the EU.

Although psychosocial risks are commonly associated with deficient working conditions, employees who have better skills are better protected. Therefore, it is important for organizations to improve working conditions and to train all workers to develop the necessary skills needed to prevent psychosocial risks.

Organizations benefit from creating partnerships and networks across economic sectors and countries to deal effectively with these questions. Involving schools and universities to educate workers in these competences is an imperative. To facilitate the process, it is important to increase synchronization between organizations and educational systems, especially universities, to better coordinate demands of competences in the labor market. To ensure success organizations and employees need to periodically identify labor market demands, taking into account current changes and identifying new competences that educational systems need to deliver to students. Moreover, psychosocial risk management should be integrated in the curricula of business schools, to deploy good practices leading to positive outcomes at individuals and organizational level (Langenham *et al.*, 2013).

Training for managers in relation to OHS management situations, including increasing economic constraints, constant change, managing employee workload against time, and managing conflicts and effective negotiation, are needed to solve challenging situations and to improve the quality of working life, increasing innovation and performance in organizations (Tappura *et al.*, 2014).

Another aspect previously mentioned is the growth of the service sector in the economy that has introduced important changes in job characteristics and work environment, increasing contact with other people. Hence, new psychosocial risks are emerging that challenge organizations to prevent them.

In the service sector, where employees' main responsibility is to produce and deliver services that customers, clients, and users demand, in addition to technical competences, the development of interpersonal relationships becomes an essential aspect of work training. Typically, in their contact with clients, employees are compelled to respond in a helpful way, even in cases of demanding clients, and it requires excellent management of emotions to do an effective job where empathy and compassion play key roles.

"Emotional labor" refers to the delivery of services where workers are expected to show emotions and feelings to accomplish tasks (Grandey, 2000). Employees have appropriate emotions in face-to-face or distant interactions and organizations manage employee activity through supervision, training, and organizational codes of ethics (Ashforth & Humphrey, 1993). On this token, excessive emotional demands have the potential to create a negative impact on health, resulting in burnout, symptoms of emotional exhaustion, detachment from others, and reduced individual performance (Maslach *et al.*, 1996).

Although motivational theories (e.g. Maslow's hierarchy of needs, Herzberg's two factor theory) have practical application, nowadays new challenges suggest that these theories need to be reviewed.

Organizational strategies frequently recommend preventing psychosocial risks, particularly in manufacturing where there are repetitive tasks lacking meaning, and including job enrichment and engagement, with better organization of teamwork and the introduction of new technologies. The growth of service industries, which is transforming economies and societies, requires new strategies to prevent the increase of psychosocial risks.

Additionally, effective management of psychosocial risks needs to integrate the macro, micro, and organizational levels across countries in the EU. At an organizational level there is a need for systematic and effective policies to prevent and manage psychosocial risk factors and enable preventive measures to improve employees' health standards. To achieve expected results and positive effects in workplaces it is important that the approaches used are adapted to converge with specific work contexts and national circumstances.

The dimensions that influence perceptions of psychosocial risks defined at the macro level often are not properly aligned with risk variables in organizations and with the diversity of stakeholders.

Planning of management and assessment of psychosocial risks include the following dimensions: organization size (considering that commonly SMEs require more assistance because they have fewer resources); sector of economic activity; workers' characteristics (gender, age, education level); position in the organization; context of the organization within the country; cultural aspects (risk sensitivity, risk tolerance); and identification of the objectives of psychosocial risk management (Leka *et al.*, 2008).

Risk management is a dynamic and cyclical process that must be adapted to fit the organization structure and demands of its external environment (Langenham *et al.*, 2013).

Psychosocial risks may be evaluated and managed based on a participatory approach that includes four steps in the model we propose next: preparation, risk assessment, implementation of interventions, and continuous evaluation to secure progress.

Phase 1: Preparation – raise awareness in the workplace – "prepare for action"

The first phase, preparation, includes all activities needed to match the type of intervention to the specific context, and to get organizational commitment to advance to the following phases (Fridrich *et al.*, 2015).

Phase one includes informing people (managers, employees, human resource managers), and forming a representative group to coordinate the project; to design an action plan with specific procedures, deadlines, responsibilities for available resources; and to communicate this plan to all members of the organization in meetings, newsletter, brochures and posters (Schaufeli, 1999).

Before initiating the program, it is crucial to involve all internal and external stakeholders, namely business owners, managers, employees, customers, about the deployment of preventive measures to ensure effective implementation. Inclusion of all parties in prevention efforts reduces barriers to change and increases effectiveness (Iavicoli *et al.*, 2011). Each member of the organization and all the social actors need to increase knowledge of the environment to be successful (Leka *et al.*, 2008).

During the action cycle phase, top and middle managers, employees, and other stakeholders receive information and training, and are consulted with to provide suggestions for improvement, opinions, or to present proposals aiming to increase participation in decision-making. All stakeholders need to understand the implementation of the process and the benefits of the intervention.

Phase 2: Risk assessment – identify hazards – "to be ready for change"

The second stage consists in a diagnosis that includes a situation analysis and risk evaluation aimed to collect information about the organizational environment and increase knowledge for the management people who work in the organization. This phase includes identification of psychosocial factors and of the most vulnerable employees, estimation of risks according to likelihood and potential severity, and planning interventions with preventive precautions.

Risk evaluation covers specific methodologies, instruments, and procedures according to the nature of risks and hazards. To identify psychosocial risks the following instruments and procedures can be used (Schaufeli, 1999; Schaufeli *et al.*, 2002): checklists (lists with work-related psychosocial risk factors); interviews (with people highly familiar with the organization structure and strategies); surveys about job characteristics, using large samples of workers; management indicators such as absenteeism, turnover, accidents, mistakes, and decreased performance; and focus groups that may include discussions with managers and employees.

These methods cover two assessment categories: (a) quantitative methods using questionnaires and surveys intended to increase reliability and validity; (b) qualitative methods using interviews and focus groups to collect information. Checklists on absenteeism and turnover collects objective data that facilitates fast assessment of psychosocial work environments. Questionnaires and interviews provide useful subjective of workers' experiences.

Furthermore, assessment of psychosocial reality of working conditions using indicators and questionnaires administered to representative samples of individuals in the organization is important. One of the most cited questionnaires is the Copenhagen Psychosocial Questionnaire (COPSOQ), developed by Kristensen *et al.* (2005). COPSOQ assesses the psychosocial work environment, including the type of production and work tasks, work content, interpersonal relations, leadership, work-individual interface, workers' health, wellbeing, and personality traits. This questionnaire is used by different organizations, industries, sectors, and countries.

COPSOQ II, a revised version, includes 41 scales and 127 items. New scales on values at the workplace added: trust, justice, and social inclusiveness. Scales on variation, work pace, recognition, work–family conflicts, items to identify offensive behavior, and new scales to assess health symptoms including burnout, stress, sleeping problems, and depressive symptoms were also added (Pejtersen *et al.*, 2010). In Spain, COPSOQ was adapted and validated as ISTAS21 (Moncada *et al.*, 2005; Moncada *et al.*, 2014).

Although awareness of workers' perceptions collected with assessment instruments is important, instruments are repetitive (e.g. questionnaires to measure stress, burnout, satisfaction, harassment, organizational climate) and their use can be more efficient when integrated in one aggregate analysis to facilitate the simultaneous assessment of multiple psychosocial risk factors.

There is great need for briefer and more concise instruments to effectively assess psychosocial risks. From the point of view of employers and employees, one evaluation instrument including various dimensions of the work environment would have more benefit to save time and financial resources (Houdmont *et al.*, 2013).

Phase 3: Planning and interventions – implementation of action plan – "what to do"

The third phase involves planning organizational change aiming to minimize problems. Here it is important to define what type of actions needs to be implemented as well as the intensity, priorities, and identification of interventions by different divisions in the organization.

The design and deployment of interventions aimed to reduce risk require an "action plan" identifying clear objectives, timing, scheduling, clear roles and responsibilities, level of involvement, resources required, identification of expected outcomes in terms of health and business, and how to measure them, identifying strengths and areas of improvement and phases of implementation.

Intervention planning must prioritize risks, including severity of risks, identifying the problems to be solved considering that priorities are influenced by costs, investment, and expected benefits (Schaufeli, 1999).

The design of the action plan has to involve all stakeholders and be disseminated throughout, raising awareness with training. Although the employer is responsible for the implementation of the plan to prevent and eliminate psychosocial risks, managers at all levels are responsible for the success of the programs in terms of employees' involvement in and commitment to the process.

Phase 4: Monitoring and evaluation of action plan

Finally, the fourth phase is based on plan implementation and monitoring, making sure that necessary adjustments for continuous improvement are secured. A comparative analysis should be made at different moments before and after measure implementation to evaluate optimal psychosocial conditions overtime and the impact of changes (Leka *et al.*, 2003).

Evaluation can be conducted at the process level to assess if the program was developed properly and according to plan, and at the result level, to measure efficiency of interventions, in terms of outcome and costs involved. It is important to conduct cost–benefit analysis comparing pre-assessment and post benefits using objective indicators.

There is a misconception that prevention programs for psychosocial risks increase costs, but in reality evidence shows that failure to address psychosocial risks in organizations increases costs for employers, workers, and societies in general (EU-OSHA, 2014b).

Knapp *et al.* (2011) report investment return of over 9 euros for every euro spent in psychosocial risk management. Another study shows that the costs in developing and implementing an intervention to diminish psychosocial risks in the Dutch police over a period of four years was estimated at 3 million, and as result psychosocial risk factors decreased 10 percent and absenteeism 3 percent, accruing to a 40 million euro savings (Houtman *et al.*, 2007). The most important thing is that employers in the EU increasingly understand that organizational performance decreases and organizational costs increase when psychosocial risk is not adequately managed.

The benefits of managing psychosocial risks and work-related stress supersede implementation costs. It is not easy to assign a monetary value to the results because it is difficult to assess health, but whenever possible indicators should be considered to demonstrate costs compatible with results in terms of efficiency.

In the final phase results need to be disseminated across the organization with the purpose to sustain motivation and commitment to secure program continuity as an essential component of long-term sustainability. This process of continuous evaluation and improvement are critical in fostering organizational learning and sustainable development (Leka *et al.*, 2011).

Psychosocial risk management at individual level interventions to manage psychosocial risks within organizations can also be carried out at individual employee level. Considering that the impact of psychosocial risks can affect employees differently depending on individual characteristics and coping mechanisms, not all employees develop the same reactions when faced with adverse situations. Different types of emotional responses are possible depending on cognitive evaluation of the situation and individual knowledge and resources.

Personality characteristics such as locus of control, self-esteem, optimism, type A personality, and other coping mechanisms influence the process. For instance, type A individuals who tend to be more competitive, with less self-control and greater impatience, have more difficulty managing stress. In contrast people with an external locus of control have higher expectations that what happens is the result of external/environmental factors which they cannot influence. People with higher internal locus of control are more likely to effectively manage psychosocial risks and optimist individuals face stress in a less negative way. Although self-esteem has not been sufficiently investigated, it is apparent that people with high self-esteem develop greater resistance to face unpleasant events. The coping style is related to actions triggered when stress/psychosocial risks are perceived, and some individuals are more successful in managing psychosocial risk than others (Parkes, 1994).

In Europe, employers are encouraged to provide psychosocial risk in the workplace through training to help employees adapt faster and be more flexible when facing disruptions and change. All seems to indicate the benefits associated with the development of employees' coping mechanisms through training and coaching to overcome difficulties and increase wellbeing at work.

Training is commonly focused on the following aspects: resilience, interpersonal relationships, time management, stress management, problem-solving, relaxation techniques, handling conflicts, responding to and coping with violence, harassment, and bullying.

Effective management of stress and psychosocial risks benefits employees in avoiding work-related harm and employers because identifying problems helps to find solutions that increase workers' commitment and job satisfaction. Preventing and managing psychosocial risks improve work environments, so workers feel more valued and satisfied, generating a positive organizational culture that improves performance and competitiveness (EU-OSHA, 2013a).

The future of psychosocial risk management

Given the volume of disturbances, and the challenges of adapting to the constant change that organizations have to face in order to attain sustainability, effective management of psychosocial risk is no longer an option; it is an imperative that brings about significant benefits to organizations, national economies, and societies.

Although the concept of psychosocial risk is not new, only recently has it become a political priority in the European Union and it is pursued to improve conditions in the workplace supported by regional policies aimed at increasing economic performance and competitiveness.

In addition to approaching psychosocial risk management from the perspective of occupational health and safety (OHS), or from the perspective of human resources management (HRM), it needs to be related closely to strategic perspectives that integrate organizational and political levels, because risk management is a dynamic and cyclical process that needs to be assessed and adapted to constantly changing organizations (Langenham *et al.*, 2013).

Political decision-makers need to assign greater importance to psychosocial risks when implementing new legislation to bridge the gap and need to offer a comprehensible definition of psychosocial risks that can apply across sectors, industries, and organizations, and benefit all stakeholders.

Models implemented in the EU should be shared across countries to avoid previous mistakes with segmented efforts. It is also important to analyze and evaluate the results of initiatives and the effectiveness of processes used in the development and implementation, identifying factors that lead to success and failure in psychosocial risk management (Leka *et al.*, 2010; Iavicoli *et al.*, 2014).

One of the major pending challenges is the need to aggregate multiple tools and questionnaires into one effective instrument of comprehensive assessment of organizational climate to measure levels of satisfaction and stress that affect psychosocial risks aiming to decrease the time and financial costs of these programs.

Short surveys are more efficient to collect information and stimulate a higher rate of response than long questionnaires when the cost of time is valuable (Houdmont *et al.*, 2013).

Innovative programs should be created and disseminated to deal with emerging challenges. The development of new initiatives requires involvement and support of internal constituencies and external stakeholders, beyond traditional groups described above. Furthermore, the combined efforts of all key stakeholders are critical in ensuring that policies and knowledge are translated into effective practices across the UE to address psychosocial risks as key priorities in the modern workplace (Leka *et al.*, 2010; Iavicoli *et al.*, 2011; Van Scheppingen *et al.*, 2012).

It is important to develop appropriate competences among all constituencies to manage psychosocial risks. At the present time, given that a pressing challenge for organizations is to increase productivity, there is a growing awareness that employees need to develop Soft Skills to develop resilience, manage emotions, improve management, and contribute to meet social responsibility (Lepeley, 2017). The educational systems (school and higher education) in countries around the world must be synchronized with the needs of skills and talent of labor markets. However, most educational institutions still underestimate the usefulness of Soft Skills and the knowledge students need to succeed in life and at work. In the future, these competences will become even more important to face emerging challenges of the twenty-first century (Lepeley, 2017).

Finally, a change in attitudes and culture is necessary to recognize threats and reconcile opportunities to improve psychosocial risk management that affect individuals, organizations, and societies worldwide.

The benefits of effective psychosocial risk management need to be highlighted above and beyond the negative consequences of psychosocial risks (Leka *et al.*, 2008; Leka *et al.*, 2015a) because commonly risk management is described only as reducing negative aspects in the workplace. Research has shown that managing psychosocial risks helps to decrease absenteeism, turnover, and job dissatisfaction, while increasing positive results such as induced innovation, and increased motivation, commitment, productivity, and quality of work, and improved workers' health. In this way managing psychosocial risks contributes significantly to foster and promote wellbeing at employee level and at organizational level.

References

Ashforth, B. E., & Humphrey, R. H. (1993). Emotional labor in service roles: The influence of identity. *Academy of Management Review*, 18(1), 88–115.

Cox, T., Griffiths, A., & Rial-Gonzalez, E. (2000). *Research on work related stress*. Luxembourg: Office for Official Publications of the European Communities.

EU-OSHA (2000). *Research on work-related stress*. Luxembourg: Office for Official Publications of the European Communities.

EU-OSHA (2007). *Expert forecast on emerging psychosocial risks related to occupational safety and health*. Luxembourg: Office for Official Publications of the European Communities.

EU-OSHA (2013a). *Campaign guide: Managing stress and psychosocial risks at work*. Luxembourg: Publications Office of European Union.

EU-OSHA (2013b). *European opinion poll on occupational safety and health*. Luxembourg: Publications Office of the European Union.

EU-OSHA (2014a), Psychosocial risks in Europe: Prevalence and strategies for prevention, Publications Office of the European Union, Luxembourg.

EU-OSHA (2014b). *Calculating the cost of work-related stress and psychosocial risks European*. Luxembourg: Publications Office of the European Union.

EU-OSHA (2016). *Second European survey of enterprises on new and emerging risks (ESENER-2)*. Luxembourg: Publications Office of the European Union.

Eurofound (2016). *Sixth European working conditions survey – Overview report*. Luxembourg: Publications Office of the European Union.

European Commission (2010). *Health and safety at work in Europe (1999–2007): A statistical portrait*. Luxembourg: Publications Office of the European Union.

Fridrich, A., Jenny, J.J., & Bauer, G.F. (2015). The context, process, and outcome evaluation model for organisational health interventions. *BioMed Research International*. 2015, 12.

Gil-Monte, P.R. (2012). Riesgos psicosociales en el trabajo y salud ocupacional [Psychosocial risks at work and occupational health]. *Revista Peruana de Medicina Experimental y Salud Publica*, 29, 2.

Grandey, A. (2000). Emotional regulation in the workplace: A new way to conceptualize emotional labor. *Journal of Occupational Health Psychology*, 5(1), 95–110.

Houdmont, J., Randall, R., Kerr, R., & Addley, K. (2013). Psychosocial risk assessment in organizations: Concurrent validity of the brief version of the management standards indicator tool. *Work Stress*, 27(4), 403–412.

Houtman, I., Jettinghoff, K., & Cedille, L. (2007). Raising awareness of stress at work in developing countries: A modern hazard in a traditional working environment. *World Health Organisation Protecting Workers Health Series*, 6.

HSE Health and Safety Executive (2017). Work-related Stress, Depression or Anxiety Statistics in Great Britain 2017. Retrieved from www.hse.gov.uk/statistics/causdis/stress/stress.pdf

Hupke, M. (2013). Psychosocial risks and workers health. EU-OSHA (European Agency for Safety & Health at Work). Retrieved from https://oshwiki.eu/wiki/Psychosocial_risks_and_workers_health

Iavicoli, S., Leka, S., Jain, A., Persechino, B., Rondinone, M., Ronchetti, M., & Valenti, A. (2014). Hard and soft law approaches to addressing psychosocial risks in Europe: Lessons learned in the development of the Italian approach. *Journal of Risk Research*, 17(7), 855–869.

Iavicoli, S., Natali, E., Deitinger, P., Rondinoni, B.M., Ertel, M., Jain, A., & Leka, S. (2011). Occupational health and safety policy and psychosocial risks in Europe: The role of stakeholders' perceptions. *Health Policy*, 1(101), 87–94.

Jain, A., Leka, S., & Zwetsloot, G. (2011). Corporate social responsibility and psychosocial risk management in Europa. *Journal of Business Ethics*, 101(4), 619–633.

Jiménez, B.M. (2011). Factores y riesgos laborales psicosociales: conceptualización, historia e câmbios actuales [Factors and occupational psychosocial risks: Concept, history and current changes]. *Medicina y Seguridad del Trabajo*, 57, 1.

Knapp, M., McDaid, D., & Parsonage, M. (2011). *Mental health promotion and prevention: The economic case*. London: Department of Health.

Kristensen, T. S., Hannerz, H., Hogh, A., & Borg, V. (2005). The Copenhagen Psychosocial Questionnaire – a tool for the assessment and improvement of the psychosocial work environment. *Scandinavian Journal of Work Environment Health*, 31(6), 438–449.

Langenham, M., Leka, S., & Jain, A. (2013). Psychosocial risks: Is risk management strategic enough in business and policy making? *Safety and Health at Work*, 4, 87–94.

Leka, (2015). Psychosocial risk management: An overview. *AFA Insurance Conference*, Stockholm. Retrieved from www.afaforsakring.se/globalassets/nyhetsrum/seminarier/afa-conference_leka-keynote.pdf

Leka, S., & Jain, A. (2010). *Health impact of psychosocial hazards at work: An overview*. Geneva: World Health Organization.

Leka, S., Cox, T., & Zwetsloot, G. (2008). The European framework for psychosocial risk management (PRIMA-EF). In S. Leka, and T. Cox (Eds.), *The European framework for psychosocial risk management* (pp. 1–16). Nottingham: I-WHO.

Leka, S., Griffiths, A., & Cox, T. (2003). *Work Organization and Stress*. Geneva: World Health Organization.

Leka, S., Jain, A., Iavicoli, S., & Di Tecco, C. (2015b). An evaluation of the policy context on psychosocial risks and mental health in the workplace in the European Union: Achievements, challenges, and the future. *BioMed Research International.*

Leka, S., Jain, A., Widerszal-Bzyl, M., Zolnierczyk-Zreda, D., & Zwetsloot, G. (2011), Developing a standard for psychosocial risk management: PAS 1010. *Safety Science*, 7(49), 1047–1057.

Leka, S., L., Jain, A., Hassard, J., & Cox, T. (2013) Managing psychosocial risks: drivers and barriers. EU-OSHA (European Agency for Safety & Health at Work). Retrieved from https://oshwiki.eu/wiki/Managing_psychosocial_risks:_Drivers_and_barriers

Leka, S., L., Jain, A., Zwetsloot, G., & Cox,T. (2010). Policy-level interventions and work-related psychosocial risk management in the European Union. *Work & Stress*, 3(24), 298–307.

Leka, S., Van Wassenhove, W., & Jain, A. (2015a). Is psychosocial risk prevention possible? Deconstructing common presumptions. *Safety Science*, 71(1), 61–67.

Lepeley, M.T. (2017). *Five Pillars of Quality Organizations and Global Sustainability*. Abingdon, UK: Routledge.

Maslach, C., Jackson, S.E., & Leiter, M.P. (1996). *Maslach Burnout Inventory: Manual* (3rd ed.). Palo Alto, CA: Consulting Psychologists Press.

Moncada, S., Llorens, C., Navarro, A., & Kristensen, T. (2005). ISTAS21: Versión en lengua castellana del cuestionario psicossocial de Copenhague (COPQOQ) [ISTAS21: the Spanish version of the Copenhagen psychosocial questionnaire (COPSOQ)]. *Archivos de Prevención de Riesgos Laborales*, 1, 18–29.

Moncada, S., Mireia, U., Molinero, E., Llorens, C., Moreno, N., Galtés, A. & Navarro, A. (2014). The Copenhagen Psychosocial Questionnaire II (COPSOQ II) in Spain – A tool for psychosocial risk assessment at the workplace. *American Journal of Industrial Medicine*, 57(1), 97–107.

Parkes, K. (1994). Personality and coping as moderators of work stress processes: models, methods and measures. *Work & Stress*, 8, (2), 110–129.

Pejtersen, J., Kristensen, T., Borg, V. & Bjorner, J. (2010). Second version of the Copenhagen Psychosocial Questionnaire. *Scandinavian Journal of Public Health*, 38(3), 8–24.

Schaufeli W.B. (1999). Evaluación de riesgos psicosociales y prevención del estrés laboral: algunas experiencias holandesas [Evaluation of psychosocial risks and prevention of work stress: some Dutch experiences]. *Revista de Psicologia del Trabajo y de las Organizaciones*, 15 (2), 147–171.

Schaufeli W.B. & Salanova, M. (2002). Cómo evaluar los riesgos psicosociales en el trabajo? [How to assess psychosocial risks at work?]. *Prevención, Trabajo y Salud*, 20, 4–9.

Tappura, S., Syvänen, S., & Saarela, K.L. (2014). Challenges and needs for support in managing occupational health and safety from managers' viewpoints. *Nordic Journal of Working Life Studies*, 4(3), 31–51.

Van Scheppingen, A., Baken, N., Zwetsloot, G., Bos, E, & Berkers, F. (2012). A value case methodology to enable a transition towards generative health management: A case study from the Netherlands. *Journal of Human Resource Costing & Accounting*, 4(1), 302–319.

Part III

Emerging forms of wellbeing

8 An entrepreneurship-based model to foster organizational wellbeing

José Manuel Saiz-Alvarez

Introduction

There is a tendency in business rankings to consider the number of billionaires in countries around the world as a measure of economic success. For instance, according to the Hurun Report, the Chinese version of Forbes, 2016 was the turning point for China with records showing that China (568) outperformed the United States (535) in the number of billionaires (Rama, 2016). And it is expected that this difference will increase fast because in 2017 the number of billionaires reached 647, among which 152 are women (Table 8.1). Moreover, more than 2,000 Chinese millionaires own more than US $300 million with a total wealth of US $2.6 trillion, equivalent to UK's GDP. Although business rankings and billionaires may link wellbeing in the workplace with money and returns to investment, mere accumulation of money and capital does not necessarily bring happiness to most people or matches principles of human centered organizations. In a global economy increasingly led by knowledge and information, accumulation of money and material goods can help on the road to attaining wellbeing, but it is a necessary condition and no longer sufficient.

For those interested in the global business ranking and balances Table 8.1 shows the fast growth of Chinese companies and sectors that until now were relatively unknown but will have increasing effect in the global economy.

But in addition to capital accumulation and growth of companies there is extensive evidence demonstrating the importance of the creation of value in human and social terms to advance the global economy. In the workplace this means the creation of value that individuals derive from harmonious work climate, empathy, work–life balance, fellowship, transparency, and loyalty, all of which contribute to the improvement of personal development in sync with organizational performance and productivity. People working and sharing these values help organizations become a pole of attraction for talent. In value-creating organizations, salary is important but less relevant than other components of organizational wellbeing.

At organizational level, the value creation argument behind social networks, social capital, and social support that improves of individual wellbeing (Lee, Chung, & Park, 2018) expedites integration of individuals and organizations with

Table 8.1 Top ten Chinese billionaires in 2017.

	Name	Age	Company	Wealth US$ bn	2016–2017 % Change
1	Xu Jiayin	59	Evergrande Real Estate Group	43	272%
2	Pony Ma Huateng	46	Tencent	37	52%
3	Jack Ma Yun & family	53	Alibaba	30	–2%
4	Yang Huiyan	36	Country Garden	24	230%
5	Wang Jianlin & family	63	Wanda	23	–28%
6	Wnag Wei	47	SF Express	22	New
7	Lin Yanhong Ma Dongmin	49 47	Baidu	19	28%
8	He Xiangjian He Jianfeng	75 50	Midea	17	47%
8	Yan Hao & family	31	China Pacific Construction	17	15%
10	Ding Lei	46	Netease	16	10%
10	Li Shufu Li Xingxing	54 32	Geely	16	261%

Source: Adapted from Pan, P. (2018), *The Hurun Global Rich List 2017*, in association with 36G.

the community and society. In this social integration process each human being has a fundamental role and responsibility to cultivate the self to attain wellbeing in order to contribute to the collective wellbeing. New models of analysis of the different dimensions of human behavior place the human being at the center of attention, strengthening the development of an emerging human centered economy.

At the micro level the human centered economy is fostering the study of happiness (Ikeda *et al.*, 2016), emphasizing need to advance a rigorous body of knowledge (Adhia, 2017), and enhance the creation of psychological capital in the workplace (Youssef & Luthans, 2010), with increased attention on factors that impact organizational climate and productivity, leading to job satisfaction and wellbeing (Aziri, 2011; Saari & Judge, 2004). These studies complement traditional economic analysis based on financial accountability and socio-economic metrics based on jobs, occupations, and education, and expand awareness on subjective variables that have direct and strong impacts on wellbeing (Lockwood *et al.*, 2018) and happiness.

Although wellbeing and happiness have been long associated with philosophy, psychology, health sciences, and job security, these are new fields of study in management and organizational development. In this respect, Lepeley (2018) considers it necessary to make a clear distinction between the concept of happiness and wellbeing. Happiness is a temporary and transient condition linked primarily with pleasant emotions and pain avoidance (hedonic, Epicurian philosophy) that may or may not led to wellbeing. Wellbeing is a long-term state that is the result of personal cultivations of systematic efforts to improve oneself first as a necessary condition to make significant contributions to improve society (eudaimonic, Aristotelian philosophy). In spite of this necessary distinction, as in any emerging field there is confusion between the concepts, and many sources still use "happiness" and "wellbeing" as synonymous terms; to this end in this chapter I use the term used in the cited sources.

At the macro level, the stages of economic development and local culture are important factors that affect happiness. At this level OECD (Organisation for Economic Co-operation and Development) consults and compounds three indexes to build the happiness construct: the Better Life Index, the Happy Planet Index developed by the New Economics Foundation, and rankings in the World Happiness Report.

In general terms these indexes consider happiness as a positive drive of labor productivity, social optimism, better work environment in the private and public sectors, higher quality of life, personal security both financially and in crime reduction, incentives for family life, and help to reduce poverty. Studies on national happiness show that human centered approaches contribute to develop more inclusive societies (Lepeley, 2017a).

Additionally, Antipina (2017) shows that people in individualistic cultures, defined by prevalence of personal efforts and goals, show higher levels of wellbeing than collectivist cultures, where individual efforts to excel are not recognized or valued enough. This is important because, in human centered organizations, failure to recognize and value individual efforts has a high potential to lead to the deterioration of working conditions.

This chapter discusses a human centered model anchored in three primary drives: Social Entrepreneurship, Labor Market, and Entrepreneurial Spirit, arguing for their positive impact on organizational sustainability and on individual, interpersonal, and solidarity behavior. The content includes examples of projects that are advancing the structural transformation of communities based on Social Entrepreneurship as a component of solidarity economies anchored in a humanistic approach of value creation to increase the wellbeing of people in two Latin American countries, Mexico and Puerto Rico.

Wellbeing: is it an inclusive concept?

Studies on wellbeing conducted by Bradburn (1969), Andrews and Whitney (1976), and Campbell, Converse, and Rodgers (1976) link wellbeing with psychology, economics, business, management, and emerging fields such as neuro-economics (Crespo, 2017; Sawe, 2017; Herrmann-Pillath, 2016; Fumagalli, 2016; Park & Woo Park, 2014), happiness economics (Adhia, 2017; Lane, 2017; Piekałkiewicz, 2017), and cross-cultural dimensions related to wellbeing (Diener & Suh, 2000). Diener (2002) defines welfare based on emotions as an evaluation of life satisfaction based on individual quality of life. In his view, wellbeing is primarily affected by emotions and moods.

Conceptually, wellbeing has two dimensions: subjective wellbeing, largely identified with happiness (Lane, 2017), and objective wellbeing based on cognitive aspects. This distinction is important because the combination of positive emotions, low levels of negative moods, personality, emotional intelligence, and religion have a positive influence on general wellbeing, the sum of eudaimonic or hedonic, achieved by the individual (Athota, 2017). Table 8.2 shows that eudaimonic wellbeing is enhanced when people feel sustained happiness, experience life purpose and can face challenges that increase personal growth (Deci & Ryan, 2000), while hedonic happiness or subjective wellbeing is based on increased pleasure and decreased pain (Carruthers & Hood, 2004).

It is important to note that happiness as defined by subjective wellbeing is temporary (Schwarz & Strack, 1999), and depends on the amount as much as the type of information the individual has in mind. Additionally, subjective wellbeing is partially based on inter-individual comparisons of the individual's standard of living and mood at the time of judgment. In fact, momentary hedonic feelings can alter the intensity of happiness felt at a certain time (Stone, Shiffman & DeVries, 1999).

According to tension-reduction theories, happiness is attained when challenges are solved, objectives are met, and human needs and goals are fulfilled (Diener, Lucas & Oishi, 2002). As a result, continuous improvement at individual level and organizational level become critical. To this end, the Kaizen method shows that, when continuous improvement is both an individual and an organizational pursuit, personal job satisfaction improves in alignment with organizational performance, leading to increased productivity and competitiveness in local, national, and global markets that impact personal trust and affiliation with the organization.

Organizational efforts to pursue continuous improvement have accelerated over time as the world adopts Industry 4.0 standards where smart factories, automated processes, machines, and robotics are linked by cyber-physical systems working in synchrony with people in work-related functions and decision-making. Full automation implies that manufacturing processes, from raw materials to

Table 8.2 Hedonic and eudaimonic wellbeing.

Eudaimonic Wellbeing (Psychological Wellbeing)	Hedonic Wellbeing (Subjective Wellbeing)
• Sense of control or autonomy • Feeling of meaning and life purpose • Competence • Personal expressiveness • Personal growth • Self-acceptance • Feelings of belongingness • Social contribution	• Presence of positive mood • Absence of negative mood • Satisfaction with various domains of life (e.g. balance work and leisure) • Global life satisfaction

Source: Carruthers & Hood (2004).

production, and from procurement to distribution and shipping, are automated digitally and mechanically (Kazutoshi, 2016). An example of this development in Mexico is displayed in the Queretaro-Guadalajara axis of economic growth that integrates automotive and aerospatial industries in Queretaro with others in the so-called Mexican Silicon Valley in Guadalajara. The project is defined by a strong entrepreneurial spirit with positive impact on social entrepreneurship and humanizing the labor market. The development of this Industry 4.0 hub in Mexico has opened new labor opportunities in highly skilled jobs in research and development, and innovation, assessed as first-order competitive advantages, where innovation is built on closely linked economic and social imperatives (Ali, 2014). In this environment wellbeing is highly correlated with job satisfaction, performance, productivity, and the competitiveness necessary to face the challenges and disruptions of the global VUCA (volatile, uncertain, complex, and ambiguous) business environment that have a significant impact on business sustainability (Lepeley, 2017a, 2017b) and Mexican sustainable development. Studies conducted by Piekałkiewicz (2017) confirm that the happiness of employees at work impacts economic outcomes with positive effects on labor performance, productivity, and organizational income and revenues.

An important aspect to keep in mind is the correlation between subjective wellbeing and the three dimensions of sociopolitical integration: social cohesion (or fragmentation), the relationship between government and citizens, and quality of life (Millán, 2016). These aspects affect individuals and organizations alike and in all productive and government sectors. In general, societies with social cohesion tend to show a higher degree of happiness, largely because population unity helps to face adversity, while fragmented societies, commonly induced by political issues or social fracture, show higher potential to limit and obstruct development and solidarity and may lead to higher social inequality.

Another aspect that affects subjective wellbeing is the relationship between government and citizens. In this respect, the deployment of the welfare state in Europe after the Second World War led to improvement of quality of living and happiness, resulting in a better relationship between governments and citizens and lower levels of political corruption.

Despite the fact that the welfare state was a solution for European countries in the twentieth century, deep changes taking place in the twenty-first century in terms of economics and demographics, including decreasing numbers of people in the workforce against an aging population, increasingly impair centralized systems and welfare states with heavier burdens on people, higher taxes, and lower levels of economic growth that translate to lower government income to cover public retirement funds. Excluding the UK and Netherlands, which have increased private funding of pension systems, and Sweden and Poland, which have established private retirement accounts, other European countries have growing unfunded retirement programs that in near future may cause major deficit problems (Lepeley, 2017b).

But, so far, the European system, supported with high level of education attained in the population, contributes to maintaining low levels of corruption.

Table 8.3 Top ten least corrupt countries in the world.

Ranking place	Country	2016 score	2015 score	2014 score	2013 score	2012 score	Region
1	Denmark	90	91	92	91	90	ECA
1	New Zealand	90	91	91	91	90	AP
3	Finland	89	90	89	89	90	ECA
4	Sweden	88	89	87	89	88	ECA
5	Switzerland	86	86	86	85	86	ECA
6	Norway	85	88	86	86	85	ECA
7	Singapore	84	85	84	86	87	AP
8	Netherlands	83	84	83	83	84	ECA
9	Canada	82	83	81	81	84	Americas
10	Germany	81	81	79	78	79	ECA
10	Luxembourg	81	85	82	80	80	ECA
10	United Kingdom	81	81	78	76	74	ECA

Note: AP (Asia Pacific), ECA (Europe and Central Asia).
Source: Adapted from Transparency International (www.transparency.org).

Consideration of corruption is important because it creates inefficiencies that obstruct development and growth, significantly hindering the wellbeing of the population. Table 8.3 shows that there are seven of the top ten least corrupt countries in the world are in Europe.

Table 8.4 shows a different situation in Latin America. According to OECD (2014), there are three categories of corruption: bribery, theft of public assets, and fraud in the form of patronage. Corruption among politicians at different administrative levels introduces high inefficiencies in the system. When corruption practices are widely spread in the social network it is difficult and costly to eradicate them, particularly when countries lack a legal system able to punish corruption. Some of the main reasons for corruption in Latin America are lack of education, which causes significant disparity of knowledge and income. Consequently, Latin America is more vulnerable to suffering corruption that induces socio-political problem that negatively impact resource allocation and the quality of life of all citizens, but particularly low income groups.

Latin American countries would accrue substantial benefits using a human centered development approach including focuses on quality improvement in education and institutional accountability at all levels and in all sectors to deter corruption and to strengthen collective prosperity and financial and commercial solvency, leading to sustainability.

Private and public organizations in Latin American and Caribbean countries that combine psychology, economics, and business management to improve wellbeing are transforming organizations inserted in Industry 4.0 standards, as it was shown above in the case of Mexico. Progress is observed in organizations in all sectors applying business policies based on corporate social responsibility

Table 8.4 Corruption in Latin America.

2016 Ranking	Country	2016 score	2015 score	2014 score	2013 score	2012 score
21	Uruguay	71	74	73	73	72
24	Chile	66	70	73	71	72
41	Costa Rica	58	55	54	53	54
79	Brazil	40	38	43	42	43
87	Panama	38	39	37	35	38
90	Colombia	37	37	37	36	37
95	Argentina	36	32	34	34	35
95	El Salvador	36	39	39	38	38
101	Peru	35	36	38	38	38
113	Bolivia	33	34	35	34	34
120	Dominican Republic	31	33	32	29	32
120	Ecuador	31	32	33	35	32
123	Honduras	30	31	29	26	28
123	Mexico	30	31	35	34	34
123	Paraguay	30	27	24	24	25
136	Guatemala	28	28	32	29	33
145	Nicaragua	26	27	28	28	29
166	Venezuela	17	17	19	20	19

Source: Adapted from 2016 Transparency International (www.transparency.org).

(CSR) linked with social entrepreneurship. The relation between social entrepreneurship and wellbeing is analyzed in the next section.

Social entrepreneurship and wellbeing

Although the existing literature on entrepreneurship mainly focuses on business-related entrepreneurship rather than social entrepreneurship, the intentions of social entrepreneurs generally differ from business oriented entrepreneurs (Pramila *et al.*, 2017). Although business and social entrepreneurship are both focused on creativity and innovation, business entrepreneurship for survival purposes needs to have an income-financial focus as an important element to attain wellbeing. On the other hand, social entrepreneurship is oriented in the collective wellbeing of the community and therefore has a great impact in developing countries with substantial social imbalances.

One of the main socioeconomic problems in developing countries is the low level of education, development, growth, income, and salaries. This complex situation often leads to extra work, wasting of time, and having to do unwanted kinds of work (Pérez, Álvarez & Castaño, 2017). The problem is more prevalent among unskilled or low skilled workers at the base of the pyramid (BoP) and middle of the pyramid (MoP) and among necessity entrepreneurs (Imas, Wilson & Weston, 2012) who lack information and do not have access to training provided by private organizations or public agencies (Rahman *et al.*, 2016).

Table 8.5 HDI top ten countries (2015 data).

Rank	Country	HDI	Rank	Country	HDI
1	Norway	0.949	5	Singapore	0.925
2	Switzerland	0.939	7	The Netherlands	0.924
2	Australia	0.939	8	Ireland	0.923
4	Germany	0.926	9	Iceland	0.921
5	Denmark	0.925	10	Canada	0.920
			10	The United States	0.920

Source: United Nations Development Programme (UNDP).

Studies show that implementation of programs and policies in social entrepreneurship provided by private organizations and NGOs increases the wellbeing of clients and the individuals working in these organizations.

Moreover, the impact of social entrepreneurship based on values helps to humanize organizations in such a way that individual wellbeing becomes as important as organizational outcomes in the generation capital and EBITDA (Earnings Before Interests, Taxes, Depreciation, and Amortization). Increasingly organizations that value people as a critical element in earning fair profits accrue higher benefits as "A Great Place to Work." In these companies employees trust their leaders more, are more engaged with their own achievements, feel prouder of their company, and enjoy their employment.

When organizations adopt social entrepreneurship values and style, wellbeing increases in tandem with increases in social impact that improves corporate reputation. These positive effects are the result of effective leaders who help their subordinates to improve, are able to identify and promote talent, form high productive teams, and motivate them constantly so that in difficult times employees do their best to solve difficult organizational situations. When social problems, behavioral or health challenges affect organizations, a social entrepreneurial style is deployed for recovery and rehabilitation techniques (Ferguson, 2016).

Table 8.5 shows the top ten countries endowed with social-based economic development and the highest UN HDI (Human Development Index). HDI integrates health (life expectancy), education, and per capita income indicators with indicators of quality of living and social fairness, expanding the economic scope of the traditional Gross National Product (GNP) to include human and social development. The UN's HDI ranking matches closely with countries that lead the ranking of the World Happiness Report (2017), namely Norway, Denmark, Iceland, Switzerland, Finland, the Netherlands, Canada, New Zealand, Australia, and Sweden (Lepeley, 2017a).

In contrast with other world regions, characteristics of countries in the European Union show high level of state regulation. Controls are substantially higher in the labor market and organizations in all sectors have to comply with strict regulations on salaries, overtime, safety, and health regulations. These regulations are imposed with an aim to improve workers' wellbeing in organizations.

Subjective wellbeing (happiness), entrepreneurship, and organizational sustainability wellbeing model

Figure 8.1 displays the three organizational wellbeing (OW) elements that shape subjective wellbeing (happiness) – namely, social entrepreneurship, entrepreneurial spirit, and labor markets. The graph shows interactions to attain organizational sustainability. Organizational Wellbeing 1 (OW1) is built on solidarity-based behavior empowered by positivism and altruism; OW2 is built on interpersonal behavior strengthened with emotional intelligence and *zoon politikon* (a reference to 350 BC and Aristotle's nature of man as a political social animal); and OW3, individual behavior is shaped by personality and spirituality.

In this context, entrepreneurship is understood as a creative tool intended for growth of wealth aligned with wellbeing in organizations and societies. The hypothesis is that countries with open economic systems that promote development and expansion of entrepreneurial activity tend to be more competitive internationally, more flexible, and better prepared to face global challenges. To develop entrepreneurial capacity countries create programs that incentivize the continuous improvement of organizational processes offering entrepreneurial training and the development of ecosystems of incubators and accelerators synchronizing and securing financial support for collaboration between public and private institutions.

Organizational sustainability

Subjective organizational wellbeing is holistic and to be sustainable needs to rest on its people with EBITDA as a subordinate business process. Organizations

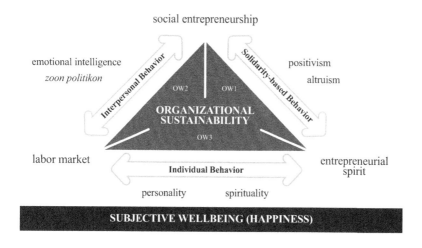

Figure 8.1 Subjective wellbeing, entrepreneurship, and organizational sustainability.
Source: Author.

that offer this work environment attract the best workers and retain loyal customers.

Organizational sustainability is the ability of an organization to provide and promote physical, psychological, and social wellbeing to workers at all levels and with different job responsibilities (Torri & Toniolo, 2010), resulting in continuous improvement of working conditions as necessary condition to attain sustainability (Lepeley, 2017b).

Social entrepreneurship is deployed through CSR (corporate social responsibility) and includes solidarity-based behavior strengthened with organizational positivism and altruism (triangle 1).

It is important to notice at this point that in today's world of economic globalization and real-time communication, global organization, regardless of sector, requires that their employees become familiar with the global environment, are willing to travel internationally, have knowledge of foreign languages, and gain international experience to fulfill organizational demands. The international experience workers gain through exchanges with people from other cultures or with diverse languages tends to improve interpersonal behavior based on trust and reciprocity.

Social integration is promoted through joy, trust, and pro-social behavior (Lane, 2017). Joy among individuals in groups is born from solidarity, interpersonal behavior, and the level of intensity of three forces that determine organizational sustainability (OW1+OW2+OW3).

To a large extent people and organizations are developing nations function in the solidarity-based behavior space guided by altruism and shared help (sector OW1). This kind of solidarity is more visible in living conditions and among low income families. Among other similar cases of social entrepreneurship programs emerging in Latin America, an example of solidarity is the Mexican program "Build your Own House" (*Échale a tu casa*) designed to incentive families to build their own houses. The program was founded in 2015 by Francesco Piazzasi and financed by the whiskey brand Chivas Regal and the multinational CEMEX (Cementos Mexicanos) to collaborate with communities and neighbors, providing funds for materials to help them build their homes. As of now, families that participated in the program have built 30,000 new houses and repaired 150,000 homes in Mexico.

In triangle OW3, individual behavior is primarily determined by interpersonal action, where people with high emotional intelligence resolve problems they face from a social perspective. It is commonly found in persons with a high capacity to manage and express emotions and handle interpersonal relationships, showing empathy, ability, and skills to manage the feelings of other people well. This interpersonal behavior arises when teams have common goals to reach and is more common in SMEs (small and medium enterprises).

In general, individual behavior is more prevalent in Anglo-Saxon and German-speaking societies than in Latin American cultures, where individual success may be correlated highly with creation of wealth. An example of this type of behavior is the listings of individual achievements, such as the rankings in Forbes 500, Who's Who in the World, or the list of billionaires in China included in Table 8.1.

Leadership and organizational sustainability

Human centered leaders have ability to acknowledge, validate, and praise the work and efforts of subordinates and help them when they demonstrate areas of improvement. For this reason, it helps significantly that managers know team members, not only professionally, but also personally, in order to continuously improve the work environment and maximize the wellbeing of the entire team. It is not easy to be a good leader, especially when organizations face surmounting challenges, but it is the leader's duty to help teams to reach targets and succeed.

To a large extent, in the current business environment it is common to see a handful of people endowed with increasing power and influence amplified by the media and information and communication technologies (ICTs), characteristic of this fourth industrial revolution. The environment is a contributing factor to dehumanizing organizations, with a high potential to convert human beings into easily replaceable assets. To avoid this problem, an increasing number of human centered organizations are focusing attention on people.

According to Goleman (1995), emotional intelligence allows people to become more aware of emotions, to understand feelings of others, tolerate work pressures and frustrations, increase capacity for empathy, improve social skills, and increase social development. Empathy and ethics are the roots of altruism that affects judgment and moral actions. When managers are empathetic, the work climate improves because they listen to and care for the wellbeing of all the people who work in the organization. This is one of the most important organizational attributes to attract the best intellectual capital, understood as the sum of human capital, structural capital, and relational capital (Saiz-Alvarez & Garcia Ochoa, 2008).

As a result, organizations move towards sustainable growth induced by supportive management, continuous improvement in customer service, and higher volume of business. Supportive management is a source of competitive advantage for firms in developing countries, where commonly the level of performance is relatively low, and opportunities are more limited to attain sustainability (Xiao *et al.*, 2018).

A combination of interpersonal, individual behavior and solidarity-based behavior was deployed in the solidarity-based project called Puerto Rico 4.0, aimed to stimulate the Puerto Rican economy with cooperatives and social entrepreneurship guided by entrepreneurial spirit focused on the labor market. The model was based on the pursuit of subjective wellbeing (happiness) where entrepreneurial spirit and work–life balance played a key role.

Conclusions

Happiness, defined as subjective wellbeing, partly determines the quality of life of executives, managers and all the people who works for the organization. In human centered organizations the human being is a central concern to participate in teams as the nuclear unit of organizations. Competent teams attract the best customers and the best talent and are loyal to the company, the products, services, and the brand they are empowered to represent. What makes the difference in human centered organizations is not only the generation of excellent EBITDA, but being able to rely on the most capable and productive people and stakeholders, and clients and investors.

Social networks accelerate change and help organizations to compete globally and increase EBITDA with less effort. But organizations need to be aware that social networks can amplify actions in the web, with the potential to help or hurt reputations. Conveying the values that support solid human centered organizations is an essential element in the global economy.

Organizations are continuously affected by global disruptions that press for constant innovation in structure and strategies, to gain resilience, renovate human and intellectual capital, and add value to talent with agility to attain continuous improvement and quality standards at all levels to attain sustainability (Lepeley, 2017b).

Subjective wellbeing can be enhanced, developing positive attitudes, promoting personal growth, purposeful lives, and work satisfaction of all the persons who work in the organization with positive relationship to become human centered leaders in an increasingly complex and competitive world.

References

Adhia, N. (2017). Happiness Economics and its Discontents, *Journal of Private Enterprise*, *32*(1), 77–88.

Ali, A.J. (2014). Innovation, Happiness, and Growth, *Competitiveness Review*, 24(1), 2–4.

Andrews, F.M., & Whitney, S.B. (1976). *Social Indicators of Well-being: American's Perceptions of Life Quality*, New York: Plenum.

Antipina, O.N. (2017). Economy, culture, and happiness: Is there interconnection? *World Economy and International Relations*, *61*(7), 35–44.

Athota, V.S. (2017). Foundations and future of well-being: How personality influences happiness and well-being, In Háša, S., & Brunet-Thornton, R. (Eds.). *Impact of Organizational Trauma on Workplace Behavior and Performance*, pp. 279–294.

Aziri B. (2011). Job Satisfaction: A Literature Review, *Management Research, and Practice*, *3*(4), 77–86.

Bradburn, N.M. (1969). *The Structure of Psychological Well-being*, Chicago: Aldine.

Campbell, A., Converse, P.E., & Rodgers, W.L. (1976). *The Quality of American Life*, New York, USA: Russell Sage Foundation.

Carruthers, C.P., & Hood, C.D. (2004). The Power of the Positive: Leisure and Well-Being, *Therapeutic Recreation Journal*, *38*(2), 225–245.

Crespo, R.F. (2017). *Economics and Other Disciplines: Assessing New Economic Currents*, Abingdon, UK: Taylor & Francis.

Deci, E.L., & Ryan, R.M. (2000). The "what" and "why" of goal pursuits: Human needs and the self-determination of behaviour, *Psychological Inquiry*, *11*, 227–268.

Deiner, E., Lucas, R.E., & Oishi, S. (2002). Subjective Well-being. The Science of Happiness and Life Satisfaction. In Snyder, C.R., & López, S.J. (Eds.) *Handbook of Positive Psychology*, Oxford, UK: Oxford University Press, pp. 63–73.

Deiner, E., & Suh, M.E. (2000). Subjective Well-Being and Age: An International Analysis, *Annual Review of Gerontology and Geriatrics*, *17*, 304–324.

Ferguson, K.M. (2016). From Victims of Market Forces to Entrepreneurs: Rethinking the Role of Supported Employment and Social Entrepreneurship in Behavioral Health Intervention, Human Service Organizations Management, *Leadership and Governance*, *40*(4), 397–409.

Fumagalli, R. (2016). Five Theses on Neuroeconomics, *Journal of Economic Methodology*, *23*(1), 77–96.

Goleman, D. (1995). *La inteligencia emocional*, 10th ed. Madrid, Spain: Javier Vergara Editor.

Herrmann-Pillath, C. (2016). Constitutive Explanations in Neuroeconomics: Principles and a Case Study on Money, *Journal of Economic Methodology*, *23*(4), 374–395.

Ikeda, S.A., Kato, H.K.B., Ohtake, F.A, & Tsutsui, Y.C. (2016). *Behavioral Economics of Preferences, Choices, and Happiness*, Tokyo: Springer Japan.

Imas, J.M., Wilson, N., & Weston, A. (2012). Barefoot Entrepreneurs, *Organization*, *19*(5), 563–585.

Kazutoshi, M. (2016). *Industry 4.0: Bringing the Human-Machine Relationship to the Next Level,* GENEX Partners.

Lane, T. (2017). How does happiness relate to economic behaviour? A review of the literature, *Journal of Behavioral and Experimental Economics*, *68*, 62–78.

Lee, S., Chung, J.E., & Park, N. (2018). Network Environments and Well-Being: An Examination of Personal Network Structure, Social Capital, and Perceived Social Support, *Health Communication*, *33*(1), 22–31.

Lepeley, M.T. (2017a). Bhutan's Gross National Happiness: An Approach to Human Centred Sustainable Development, *South Asian Journal of Human Resources Management*, *4*(2), 174–184.

Lepeley, M.T. (2017b). *Human Centered Management. 5 Pillars of Organizational Quality and Global Sustainability.* Abingdon, UK: Routledge.

Lepeley, M.T. (2018). Wellbeing and Sustainability. Advancing a Framework for Organizations Assessment and Improvement. In Lepeley, M.T., & Ochoa, P. (Eds.). *Human Centered Management. A Global View. From Personal Wellbeing to Organizational Sustainability*, Routledge. In press.

Lockwood, T., Coffee, N.T., Rossini, P., Niyonsenga, T., & McGreal, S. (2018). Where do you live influence your socio-economic status? *Land Use Policy*, *72*, 152–160.

Millán, R. (2016). Sociopolitical Dimensions of Subjective Wellbeing: The Case of Two Mexican Cities. In Rojas, M. ed. *Handbook of Happiness Research in Latin America*. Springer.

OECD (2014). *Issues Paper on Corruption and Economic Growth*, Paris, France: OECD.

Pan, P. (2018). *The Hurun Global Rich List 2017*, Pekin, China: Hurun & 3G.

Park, J.W., & Woo Park, J. (2014). How Can Neuroeconomics Unravel CSR? In *The True Value of CSR: Corporate Identity and Stakeholder Perceptions*, Palgrave-Macmillan, 280–293.

Pérez Zapata, O., Álvarez Hernández, G., & Castaño Collado, C. (2017). Engagement and/or Work Intensification, Choice and/or Obligation [*written in Spanish*, Compromiso y/o Intensificación del Trabajo. ¿Opción y/o Obligación?], *Política y Sociedad, 54*(3), 707–732.

Piekałkiewicz, M. (2017). Why do economists study happiness? *Economic and Labour Relations Review, 28*(3), 361–377.

Pramila, R., Rizal, A.M., Kamarudin, S., & Husin, M.M. (2017). Motivating Factors Contributing to Young Social Entrepreneurs' Intention to Start Social Activities, *Advanced Science Letters*, *23*(4), 2787–2790.

Rahman, S.A., Amran, A., Ahmad, N.H., & Taghizadeh, S.K. (2016). Enhancing the Wellbeing of Base of the Pyramid Entrepreneurs through Business Success: The Role of Private Organizations, *Social Indicators Research*, *127*(1), 195–216.

Rama, B. (2016). The New Millionaires are Chinese, and They Are Occupied [*written in Spanish*, Los nuevos millonarios son chinos y están ocupados], *El Español*, March , p. 8.

Saari, L.M., & Judge, T.A. (2004). Employee Attitudes and Job Satisfaction, *Human Resources Management*, *43*(4), 395–407.

Saiz-Alvarez, J.M., & García-Ochoa, M. (2008). Outsourcing and Joint-ventures in the New Knowledge Economy [*written in Spanish*, Externalización de servicios y alianzas estratégicas en la nueva economía del conocimiento], *Economía Industrial*, *370*, 135–141.

Sawe, N. (2017). Using Neuroeconomics to Understand Environmental Valuation, *Ecological Economics*, 135, 1–9.

Schwarz, N., & Strack, F. (1999). Reports of Subjective Well-being: Judgmental Processes and Their Methodological Implication. In Kahneman, D., Diener, E., & Schwarz, N. (Eds.). *Well-Being: The Foundations of Hedonic Psychology*, New York: Russell Sage Foundation, 61–84.

Stone, A.A., Shiffman, S.S., & DeVries, M.W. (1999). Ecological Momentary Assessment. In Kahneman, D., Diener, E., & Schwarz, N. (Eds.). *Well-Being: The Foundations of Hedonic Psychology*, New York: Russell Sage Foundation, 26–39.

Torri, P., & Toniolo, E. (2010). Organizational Wellbeing: Challenge and Future Foundation [*written in Italian*, Benessere organizzativo: sfide e fondamenti del futuro], *Giornale Italiano di Medicina del Lavoro ed Ergonomia*, *32*(3), 363–367.

Xiao, C., Wang, Q., van der Vaart, T., & van Donk, D.P. (2018). When Does Corporate Sustainability Performance Pay Off? The Impact of Country-Level Sustainability Performance, *Ecological Economics*, *146*, 325–333.

Youssef, C.M., & Luthans, F. (2010). An Integrated Model of Psychological Capital in the Workplace. In Lindley, P.; Harrington, S., & Garcea, N. (Eds.). *Oxford Handbook of Psychological Capital in the Workforce*, Oxford, UK: Oxford University Press.

9 Wellbeing challenges of millennials

South Africa's "Born Free" generation

Linda Ronnie

Introduction

No organization today can claim to be immune to the deep shifts in technological, economic, political, and social spheres. One of these important shifts affects the new generation entering the labor market who are eager to have a voice on matters that impact their personal and professional lives. The case is important because literature indicates significant differences in outlook, expectations, and work relationships between this and previous generations (Arsenault, 2004; Erickson, 2008; Shandler, 2009; Tapscott, 2009; Meister & Willyerd, 2010). Differences between generational cohorts, among others, include attitudes towards careers, the emphasis placed on training and development, and the need for meaningful work (Chartered Institute of Personnel Development, 2016).

In the South African context, this younger cohort is known as the "Born Free" generation (Mattes, 2011) because, on one hand, they were born after the transition to democracy but, on the other, they are also affected by practices of the past. "Born Frees" make up close to 40 percent of the 56 million people in South Africa, but there is a substantial level of unemployment in this cohort. Among the economically active population only 33 percent of men and 25 percent of women have regular employment (Kane-Berman, 2015).

One of the consequences of South Africa's apartheid legacy was an education system that did not provide the same levels of quality and access to education across race and class. Horwitz (2013) described the paradox of the South Africa labor market as an "over-abundance of low skilled employees and a shortage of intermediate and high skilled individuals."

Although the country has one of the highest rates of education expenditures in Africa, around 6.5 percent of GDP (South African National Treasury, 2015) and, despite gains made in the last 20 years, many pending educational challenges impact the supply of skilled workers to the South African economy necessary to meet the demands of today's labor force.

The education system itself is at the root of many problems as it struggles to overcome years of apartheid neglect and dysfunction due to problems with underfunding and poorly trained teachers in racially marginalized sections of the community (Breier 2009; Mattes, 2011).

So today organizations in the private and public sector face surmounting challenges attracting, motivating, and retaining the limited pool of skilled individuals to fill a fast-growing demand for labor. In this environment the participation and contribution of younger high-skilled workers is critical for businesses and organizations that rely on the talent of employees to increase productivity, competitive advantage, and organizational sustainability (Todericiu, et al, 2013; Lepeley, 2017). As South African companies are increasingly compelled to become productive to compete in the global economy, this implies high reliance on skilled workers able to foster innovation to attain continuous productivity improvement.

Highly skilled workers in the workplace are a key component in fostering national economic development, and inclusive societies, and are a condition of meeting the national need to compete globally.

However, traditional standards are hard to change. Thompson and Gregory (2012) suggest that the management style that influences hiring and retention of this cohort of employee needs to be more flexible to adjust to emerging labor force constituencies and needs to effectively recognize the expectations of skilled young employees entering the labor force.

This chapter discusses the challenges of attracting, motivating, and retaining graduates of the "Born Free" generational cohort of employees in a working environment struggling with deep change while simultaneously ensuring an organizational culture of encouragement and flexibility necessary to foster wellbeing in the workplace and sustainable development.

Generations in the South African context

Generation is defined as a distinguishable group that "shares birth interval, location, and significant life events at critical development stages" (Kupperschmidt, 2000). Mannheim defines the generation concept as "a cohort of individuals born and raised within the same historical and social context, who share a common worldview" (cited in Lyons *et al.*, 2005). Socio-political and cultural events shape boundaries of generational cohorts (Colakoglu & Caligiuri, 2010; Rasch & Kowshe, 2010) and influence attitudes and values of individuals within the group. These values and attitudes affect individual personal and professional lives.

While generational descriptions commonly apply across countries, particular characteristics of generations in developed countries can differ from those of developing countries. South Africa has unique differences due to the apartheid regime that controlled the country between 1948 and the early 1990s because people of different races were affected in various ways and different generational outlooks exist between black and white South Africans due to dissimilar upbringing and experiences. Table 9.1 shows how Deal *et al.* (2010) explain differences in generational cohorts in South Africa compared to the US and the UK (see Table 9.1).

Before an in-depth description of the "Born Free" generation is provided below, a brief discussion on the other South African cohorts is useful for clarity. The

Table 9.1 Generational cohorts' comparison of the US, UK, and South Africa.

US	Baby Boomers [1946–1963]	Generation X [1964–1979]	Generation Y / Millennials [1980–2000]	
UK	Baby Boomers [1946 – 1960]	Generation X [1960–1979]	Generation Y / Millennials [1980–2000]	
SOUTH AFRICA	Apartheid Generation [1938–1960]	Struggle Generation [1961–1980]	Transition Generation [1981–1993]	"Born Free" Generation [1994–2000]

Adapted from Deal *et al.* (2010, p. 283).

Apartheid generation (1938–1960) has no national memory prior to the institutionalization of apartheid and its legal system enforcing racial segregation. While all races in this generation were exposed to protest action and ramifications, black South Africans were more politically and socially aware (Deal *et al.*, 2010). The material conditions under which the various racial groups existed shaped their outlook on life and consequently racialized relationships in the workplace.

The Struggle generation (1961–1980) was given this name because it was characterized by countrywide protests that gripped the country in the mid-1970s. The majority of the oppressed participated in some form of resistance while many of the white population, especially white men who were conscripted into the army and Defence Force to fight against the struggle for freedom, were silent and often complicit in actions against the black majority.

The Transition generation (1981–1993) entered adolescence in the post-democratic period and retained memory of the apartheid regime. Due to recurrent educational problems, this generation experienced high levels of unemployment and similar levels of economic and physical insecurity as prior generations (Deal *et al.*, 2010). Although the Transition generation in South Africa parallels with Generation Y in the US and the UK, this chapter is focused on the unique characteristics of the younger generation cohort born in the post-apartheid period who are identified as "Born Free".

The South African millennials or "Born Free" generation[1]

People born between 1994 and 2000 in South Africa have no memory of the restrictive apartheid structures forced upon previous generations, and they live and work without official limitations (Mattes, 2011). While this generation is defined largely as black due to current demographics, it is believed that young South Africans across the color line enjoy more in common with each another than previous generations in the country (Martins & Martins, 2010).

As a result of being born outside the limitations of racial segregation, the "Born Free" cohort is more culturally integrated with others in their generation (Malila, 2015). However, it needs to be acknowledged that the "Born Free" label faces challenges because many think that this name is more aspirational than real and less homogenous than indicated (Maphunye *et al.*, 2014). For the purposes of this discussion, tensions are acknowledged, showing this contested term in quotation marks.

Although South Africans in the Millennial generation have faced a diversity of experiences, they hold similar beliefs around the world, especially with other individuals in this generation in other developing countries who face similar challenges such as inequality, political instability, financial volatility, high birth rates, and similar demography. And from these dimensions they differ from people in the Generation Y of developed countries. For example, a large proportion of skilled employed black Millennials support their extended family, following cultural expectations. On the other hand, Millennials in South Africa, as in developed countries, are more proficient in technology than previous generations and use social media collaboratively to solve problems that enable innovation (Burrows, 2013). Millennials are less risk-averse, another factor that may have a positive spinoff for organizations.

Furthermore in contrast with previous generations Millennials show a particularly proactive attitude towards career paths, emphasizing training and development, and the need for meaningful work (Kim 2008).

Accenture reports that it is young South African employees' loyalty is self-directed and they prefer diverse and flexible work arrangements with appropriate salaries (Burrows, 2013). "Born Frees" are more driven by challenging tasks and a desire for new things (Parry *et al.*, 2010). And their diverse approaches to work create new and different challenges with high implications for all kinds of organizations in the private and public sectors.

The work environment in South Africa

South Africa is still recovering from unique historical circumstances rooted in inequalities that hinder growth in employment and impact the educational sectors (Horwitz *et al.*, 2006), including shortcomings of national training facilities and the Sector Education and Training Authorities (SETAs). The accumulation of these deterring events generates particular challenges for employers and the workforce.

South African organizations face surmounting challenges to find talented and skilled employees in a limited pool (McKechnie & Bridgens, 2008). Meanwhile, forward-thinking organizations try to outsmart competitors seeking young employees using "people management differentiation" (Markova & Ford, 2011) to attract talented individuals, motivate them to attain high productivity, and retain them in the organization as a fundamental business priority.

Challenge 1: Attraction factors: what counts for Millennials?

The reputation of employers is an essential factor to attract job applicants to specific positions when they seek additional information about an organization (Collins, 2006). The value of reputation or a recognized brand are competitive edges notorious in South Africa (Moroko & Uncles, 2008) as a worldwide and critical factor that yields benefits as a preferred source of employability. Organizations that show commitment to improving the internal as much as the external environment attract Millennials seeking to match values of their own. Millennials who seek to make meaningful contributions to an organization, while remaining true to themselves, are drawn to these organizations.

Beyond remuneration and income, the prospects of career growth, work/life balance, strong sense of purpose, investment in and use of technology, opportunity to travel, and professional development, are all factors that attract young people to organizations (Deloitte, 2016).

As a consequence of the skilled shortage mentioned earlier, young talented South Africans are in the unique position of choosing an employer based on their specific criteria rather than settling for "just a job". South African organizations face a dual challenge to compete with other organizations for talent and to offer a high level of mobility to Millennials within the workforce (Bussin & Moore, 2012).

Organizational solutions

Drawing from strategies deployed by successful global organizations to attract highly skilled Millennials, South African employers are making adjustments in recruitment and organizational work climate to include preferences of the young generation (Howe & Strauss, 2000; Erickson, 2008) that include (1) communication about the what and how; and (2) the i-deal proposition.

1. COMMUNICATION – THE WHAT AND HOW

As was previously stated, Millennials are attracted to organizations with good reputation, intensive use of technology, and access to continuous growth and development. Reputation matters to Millennials and when they have the opportunity to choose between organizations, recognition and prestige become central factors. Therefore, more organizations need to ensure that their public profiles are regularly updated with key messages attractive to Millennials. Beyond website updates, webmasters must be aware of current trends and social media like LinkedIn, Facebook, and Twitter that encourage job applications, given that online job searching is among the most popular recruitment methods. In addition, organizations need to develop social recruiting platforms with relevant data that provide an insider's view of organizational culture using videos and snapshots showing activities of young employees during work days (Moye, 2013).

Millennial employees can also help as recruiters of new talent. These referrals can occur through employees sharing job vacancies via social networks, advertising growth opportunities, and promoting future and ongoing training and development. One of the key attractions for Millennials is certainty that their chosen organization will continue to show interest in their continuous learning capacity. Ongoing training and development is an area "Born Frees" demand as part of the employment package and career development and includes partial or full study reimbursement (Bussin & van Rooy, 2014).

An effective source of applicants and talent search is embedded in strategic alliances between job provider organizations, the workforce, and educational institutions. This is a partnership that facilitates necessary input in curriculum development and helps advisory committees to synchronize graduates' skills and competences demanded in the workforce, sponsor graduate career fairs to inform people about organizations' profile, and study reimbursement fringe benefits for high achievers, high school students, and graduates.

2. AN I-DEAL VALUE PROPOSITION

The notion of idiosyncratic deals (or i-deals) underpins the customized employee value proposition. An i-deal "grants workers preferred employment condition(s) and helps employers attract, motivate, and/or retain highly valued contributors," (Rousseau *et al.*, 2009). Typically, employees negotiate conditions that satisfy personal needs and preferences of applicants. An example of an i-deal is the salary structure, which is an important factor for Millennials. Young employees need assurance that the organization offers a suitable base remuneration consistent with benchmarking standards and allows progression in the organization. Meanwhile pension funds and investment share schemes seem to be less attractive to "Born Frees" than bonuses and cash incentives (Bussin & van Rooy, 2014).

I-deals are important because they offer win-win employment situations that encourage organizations to customize people's management strategies. Employers need innovative ways to attract skilled "Born Free" applicants and the introduction of i-deals help organizations that face fierce competition for skilled employees. I-deals have shown a positive impact on organizational commitment that plays a significant role in employees' motivation and retention (Ng & Feldman, 2010).

Challenge 2: Motivating and engaging Millennials

Two areas require special attention to engage Millennials with their work: (a) provision of regular performance feedback and clarity of career development paths, and (b) explicit and meaningful performance recognition. Frequent and effective communication is at the heart of these concerns for Millennials. Most of them seek ongoing reassurance that they are valued through frequent feedback, and they appreciate managers who are supportive and nurturing as leaders (Weick, 2003; Weick *et al.*, 2002).

Although Millennials seek increasing involvement with work and the organizational environment, this is a subtle consideration that requires good balance between work demands without overwhelming young employees with a high volume of tasks, negatively impacting on personal life. Although in the short term this may not seem an important issue for new employees, symptoms of increasing stress and burnout require fast attention because in general this generation places greater importance on work–life balance than previous generations (Zemke *et al.*, 2000; Smola & Sutton, 2002).

Furthermore, Millennials need personal support from organizational leaders well equipped with skills to help them to manage projects effectively and make the decisions necessary to deliver expected results (Chartered Management Institute, 2008).

Organizational solutions

Core messages from employers to employees need to address personal development, opportunities for advancement, mentorship and training, organizational responsibility, challenging work, meaningful engagement, constant feedback, and work–life balance (Allen, 2004; Martin, 2005; Terjesen *et al.*, 2007; Shaw & Fairhurst, 2008; Hurst & Good, 2009; Thompson & Aspinwall, 2009) deployed in practice through (1) frequent appraisals, (2) motivating employees with incentives they value, and (3) rotation programs that allow them to experience different divisions of the organization.

1. FREQUENT APPRAISALS

Open Box Software, a South African software company specializing in the development of innovative solutions, is a practical example. Malcolm Hall, co-founder of Open Box, wanted to start a business that provided incentives for employees to happily go to work every day. The company features a flat organizational structure based on open communication policies with a focus on a collegial environment (Metcalf, 2011). A unique aspect of their people management practice is its appraisal process. Employees receive feedback on a weekly basis. Junior employees' feedback is focused on development of individual skills, technical issues that arose during the assessment period, and improvements necessary in the future. This is in contrast to senior employees where feedback is less technical and focused on broader concerns that include entire project plans, project specifications, communication and interpersonal skills, and performance evaluation. The type of approach used by Open Box Software leads to highly committed staff and can be applied in all industries and sectors (Lepeley, 2017; Metcalf, 2011).

Growing numbers of prominent global organizations are abandoning traditional performance assessment systems that are becoming obsolete and are replacing them with frequent performance feedback aimed to incentivize employee engagement leading to performance improvement (Lepeley, 2017). These initiatives resonate with Millennials interested in high engagement integrated with ongoing feedback from managers.

2. MOTIVATE EMPLOYEES WITH MEANINGFUL INCENTIVES

In general "Born Frees" prefer recognition for service awards and other forms of non-monetary incentives as a priority (Bussin & van Rooy, 2014). Parry *et al.* (2010) found that South African Millennials rate achievement, work–life balance, and self-actualization as key measures of career success. Therefore, it makes sense for organizations to offer appropriate rewards. Team-based projects that allow Millennials to lead generational cohorts also instil a sense of achievement and provide opportunity to develop highly sought job experiences for young employees.

3. ROTATION PROGRAMS ALLOW MILLENNIALS TO EXPERIENCE DIFFERENT SECTORS OF ORGANIZATIONS

A prime example of how rotation programs deliver good results comes from Brazil, another developing country. Semco is a Brazilian manufacturing company that offers new employees the opportunity to gain experience in all departments and cross-functional areas prior to making a final employment choice. On a regular basis, employees are encouraged to change jobs in the company (Garcia, 2013), a method that provides all employees the opportunity to learn new skills. Semco accrues benefits guaranteeing a supply of multi-skilled employees for different operations. The motivational component of providing job alternatives to Millennials is valued because of their desire to perform meaningful work (Ng *et al.*, 2010).

Challenge 3: Retention strategies for Millennials

Millennials commonly show a lower level of allegiance to their employer but higher levels of loyalty to their work and peers. When problems arise in the workplace, the highly skilled young workers are more inclined to leave the employer than to stay. Deloitte (2016) points out that one out of four Millennials would leave their current organization during the next year given the choice. This number rises to 44 percent when the time span increases to two years. This is a serious challenge to South African organizations employing large numbers of "Born Frees."

Millennials in developing countries show lower loyalty to current employers. While 76 percent of young South Africans reported themselves as considering leaving their organizations in the next five years, Chile reports 71 percent, South Korea 74 percent, Colombia 75 percent, India 76 percent, and Peru 82 percent. And one of the main reasons for leaving an organization is the lack of modern leadership skills (Deloitte, 2016). This need for leadership skills may explain increasing enrolment in graduate programs such as a Master's degree in Business Administration (Ronnie & Wakeling, 2015).

Millennials in South Africa show a preference for rapid career mobility even if it means changing jobs frequently. Career progression is focused on advancement opportunities but extends to progression and how well organizational prospects and advancement are presented to them. Securing career and developmental opportunities are important for young employees because they are starting their career (Hess & Jepsen, 2009). Skilled Millennials are highly sought after in South Africa and abroad, where opportunities for exchange and acquisition of new knowledge exist through many alternatives available of employment options (Breier, 2009).

Mobility concerns pressure young employees "to differentiate themselves in terms of developing distinctive competencies and generating options to pursue personal and career goals" (Rousseau, 2001) and therefore retention of "Born Free" employees is a challenging endeavor. Given the high costs associated with job rotation and recruitment, it makes financial sense for employers to deploy effective retention programs. The shortage of talent, the "brain drain" led by young employee mobility, plus the retirement of Baby Boomers, is increasingly challenging for organizations in a precarious position regarding the pipeline of suitably skilled employees.

Organizational solutions

The suggestions offered to organizations regarding motivation of Millennials also apply to retention imperatives. Additional advice for organizations to expedite turnover challenges and advance standards of sustainability includes leadership training and the development of alternative lattice career paths namely:

1. SUPPORT AND TRAINING FOR MILLENNIALS INTERESTED IN LEADERSHIP ROLES

Coupled with training and development initiatives, young people should be encouraged, in addition to lattice career paths, to climb the organizational ladder and reach senior positions. Organizations wishing to retain young employees must support their ambitions and interests in professional development.

Millennials appreciate primarily two aspects of the mentoring process: (a) quality / effectiveness of advice received (94 percent) and (b) the mentor's interest in their professional development (91 percent) (Deloitte, 2016). The opportunity to have someone to ask for advice and assist in the development of leadership skills is keenly felt by "Born Free" employees and Millennials in the workforce in developing countries. Business schools can also play a meaningful role in assisting companies in developing required management skills and improving competencies for successful mentorship.

2. CREATE ALTERNATIVE CAREER PATHS IN ADDITION TO TRADITIONAL LINEAR EXPECTATIONS

Organizations can fulfil Millennials' interests with high awareness of their needs and desires in terms of career progression including lateral / lattice career moves (Wilson *et al.*, 2008). Lateral moves provide opportunity for a wider range of career paths with potential to expand personal satisfaction, offer new career trajectories, and open prospects to undertake further professional challenges within their organizations (Helvey, 2016).

Millennials show eagerness to move on when there is the clear possibility to learn something new, be involved in substantial change, and be able to contribute meaningfully (Hobart & Sendek, 2014). The use of the lattice strategy of horizontal career paths may enhance engagement and loyalty of young employees and allow the organization to differentiate from competitors.

Challenge 4: Dealing with the generational mix

South Africa needs to develop effective strategies to manage the expectations of skilled employees entering the workforce and capitalize on the "Born Free" generation's potential to optimize their contribution. To achieve this objective, it is necessary to understand particular characteristics of all the generations in the workforce including Generation X and Baby Boomers as employee cohorts that have different needs and expectations but today share the same workplace. Generational differences pose surmountable challenges that organizations must manage effectively to create a harmonious, cohesive, and efficient working climate that can integrate different generations in the same context (Dols *et al.*, 2010).

One of the main challenges for organizations with Baby Boomer managers and Generation X co-workers is the need to balance work demands with the desires of Millennials willing to make meaningful contributions based on their level of competency. Managers play a critical role developing – or breaking – psychological contracts with Millennial employees. Psychological contracts underpin employer–employee relationships based on perceptions of the different parties' commitment to each other (Chartered Institute of Personnel Development, 2016). A breach of the psychological contract can cause irreparable damage to work relationships and result in employees withholding effort or resigning from the job (Conway & Briner, 2005). South Africa's current skills shortage introduces additional constraints that negatively impact productivity.

Organizational success hinges on effective and well synchronized collaboration between individuals of different generations in the workplace despite differences between generational groups. For example, Van der Walt and du Plessis (2010) reported that Baby Boomers prefer teamwork where they are in charge, while Generation X members favor teams where individual contribution is valued, and Millennials enjoy teamwork but require some supervision.

It must also be clarified that the perceptions of Baby Boomers who worked during the apartheid years can be quite different from those who joined the workforce in the era of democracy (Shrivastava *et al.*, 2014). Lloyd *et al.* (2011) warn that policies implemented to redress past imbalances – such as employment equity – have triggered challenges in the South African workplace. Compliance with legislation requires targets related to recruitment, retention, training, and development of different groups identified as black people, women, and people with disabilities (Republic of South Africa, 1998 [Employment Equity Act]). A key objective of this Act is to achieve a diverse labor force.

A recent study showed that Millennials agreed that the affirmative action law is necessary and enhances autonomy in the workplace (Mula, 2014). Although this is encouraging, the implementation of legislation must be supported by positive employment practices that focus on progressive people practices that can introduce real changes in organizational culture (Booysen, 2007).

Regardless of differences between generations along values, motivations, and attitudinal beliefs, organizations must harness and deal with differences, tensions, and conflict, through implementing inclusionary practices. These strategies should diversify the workforce to attain necessary levels of innovation and continuous performance improvement inherent with employees' satisfaction to increase productivity and competitiveness at the local, national, and global levels.

Organizational solutions

Three key recommendations for organizations dealing with inter-generational challenges are suggested below: building collaborative relationships, cross-generational mentoring, and rethinking people management strategies.

1. BUILDING COLLABORATIVE RELATIONSHIPS

One way to improve collaboration in organizations is focusing on shared values. In South Africa, forward-looking organizations are drawing on the concept of *ubuntu,* an old African philosophy that has gained increasing attention. The revival of this practice may be understood as "an attempt to (re) discover African cultural values eroded by colonialism and apartheid" (Beet & Le Grange, 2005). *Ubuntu* is embracing the value of generosity, hospitality, friendliness, care, and compassion among human beings (Tutu, 2000). Tutu explained that individuals who share these values are willing to support others and strengthen themselves. In organizational settings, Mbigi (2000) described five key values underpinning *ubuntu*:

- survival (sustainability)
- compassion (helping others)
- solidarity (being part of a collective)
- dignity
- respect (courtesy, organizational citizenship, and consideration).

Practicing *ubuntu* involves strategies to build and consolidate relationships between groups in the workplace. The adoption of the *ubuntu* philosophy leads to the strengthening of organizational culture and promotes the formation of an identity where everyone acts in the interests of the self and in high synchronicity with interests of the team to achieve the organization's objectives. Anyone who values herself/himself is able to value and support the interests of others. These are also fundamental principles in human-centered management (Lepeley, 2017). This unified identity is crucial in filling gaps created by South Africa's fractured past.

Promoting tolerance using *ubuntu* through a variety of methods in organizations empowers employees, offers independence, and strengthens inter-dependence. These actions lead to increased employee participation, level of work satisfaction, and engagement where all employees – across generational groupings – assume responsibility for their actions and outputs. This comes about through participative leadership that enhances understanding across generations, gender, race, and culture (Lepeley, 2017). Effective employee training programs with continuous assessment of results is the best way to lead organizations into meaningful interactions. Shrivastava *et al.* (2014) suggest inclusive communication among leaders and employees as vital, using actions as showing genuine sensitivity to individual concerns, enhancing self-esteem, and using win-win conflict resolution strategies to consolidate the success of *ubuntu* cultures.

2. CROSS-GENERATIONAL ACTIVITIES

Organizations in all industries and sectors should create opportunities for cross-generational mentoring to promote knowledge transfer among employees and increase work satisfaction that benefits all participants, including Millennials who seek new knowledge and Baby Boomers who wish to share experiences gained over time.

But today there are instances that reverse cases, where Baby Boomer and Generation X employees are mentored by Millennials familiar with the latest technology. "Reverse mentoring" can be an effective approach to shifting attitudes to benefit organizations. A related activity consists in integrating cross-generational teams to participate in joint volunteer activities that help to engage Millennials with their inherent desire to be productive citizens, serve society, and work for organizations with good ethical records. Generation X, who enjoy goal-directed activities, and Baby Boomers, committed to a track record of giving back through social initiatives, help organizations improve productivity and social inclusiveness. Organizations that show interest in giving back to society and supporting these initiatives reinforce their reputational standing and are attractive for Millennials.

3. RETHINKING PEOPLE MANAGEMENT STRATEGIES

A UK report offers several recommendations to address productivity in inter-generational workplaces (CAP, 2008) that include consideration of radical changes in terms of flexible working practices rather than presentation of a generic value proposition. Another proposition is to have conversations with employees to assess their views and motivations and involve them in the development of plans to improve people management practices. Often, each generational cohort believes they bring unique strengths to the workplace and organizations need to identity areas of commonality and the strengths of each group, and build on them to ensure diversity with inclusion unifying practices.

What's next for Millennials and managers?

Business and organizations in the private and public sector benefit and advance on the road to wellbeing, acknowledging the expectations of skilled employees entering the workforce. South Africa can capitalize the potential of the "Born Free" generation and optimize their contribution with continuous assessment of their needs and those of all employees. Continuous improvement of organizational culture as a base for human-centered management creates best opportunities for employees' development and engagement, leading to optimal service for customers aligned with increases in individual performance and the organizational competitiveness required to attain sustainability in a complex and highly integrated world. The changes and challenges that affect organizations today, in developing and developed countries, are profound and broad based. The challenges for Millennials, as much as for workers of all other generations, depend increasingly on human ability and a commitment to deploy the *ubuntu* philosophy, anchored in the principles and practices discussed above, as a necessary condition for the optimal synchronization of wellbeing at personal, organizational, social, national, and global levels.

Note

1. These terms are used interchangeably in this chapter.

References

Allen, P. (2004). Welcoming Y. *Benefits Canada*, 28(9), 51–54.

Arsenault, P.M. (2004). Validating generational differences: A legitimate diversity and leadership issue. *The Leadership & Organization Development Journal,* 25(2), 124–141.

Beet, P., & Le Grange, L. (2005). 'Africanising' assessment practices: Does the notion of Ubuntu hold any promise? *South African Journal of Higher Education*, 19(S), 1197–1207.

Booysen, L.L. (2007). Societal power shifts and changing social identities in South Africa: Workplace implications. *South African Journal of Economic and Management Sciences,* 10(1), 1–20.

Breier, M. (2009). Introduction. In J. Erasmus & M. Breier (Eds.). *Skills shortages in South Africa: Case studies of key professions* (pp. 1–21). Cape Town: HSRC Press.

Burrows, (2013, August). *Managing the millennial gap.* Retrieved from https://mg.co.za/article/2013–08–30–00-managing-the-millennial-gap/

Bussin, M., & Moore, A. (2012). Reward preferences for generations in selected information and communication technology companies. *South African Journal of Human Resource Management*, 10(1).

Bussin, M., & Van Rooy, D.J. (2014). Total rewards strategy for a multi-generational workforce in a financial institution. *South African Journal of Human Resource Management, 12*(1).

Chartered Institute of Personnel Development (2008). *Gen Up: How the four generations work.* Retrieved from www.cipd.co.uk/subjects/dvsequl/general/_genup.htm.

Chartered Institute of Personnel Development (2016). *The psychological contract.* Retrieved from www.cipd.co.uk/hr-resources/factsheets/psychological-contract.aspx

Chartered Management Institute (2008). *Generation Y: Unlocking the talent of young managers.* Chartered Management Institute.

Colakoglu, S., & Caligiuri, P. (2010). Cultural influences on Millennial MBA students' career goals: Evidence from 23 countries. In Ng, E., Lyons, S. & Schweitzer, L. (Eds). *Managing the New Workforce* (pp. 262–280). Cheltenham: Edward Elgar.

Collins, C. (2006). *The interactive effects of recruitment practices and product awareness on job seekers' employer knowledge and application behaviour.* Ithaca, NY: Center for Advanced Human Resource Studies (CAHRS), Cornell University ILR School.

Conway, N., & Briner, R.B. (2005). *Understanding psychological contracts at work: A critical evaluation of theory and research.* London: Oxford University Press.

Deal, J., Stawiski, S., Graves, L., Gentry W., Ruderman, M., & Weber, T. (2010). Perceptions of authority and leadership: A cross-national, cross-generational investigation. In Ng, E., Lyons, S., & Schweitzer, L. (Eds.), *Managing the New Workforce* (pp. 281–306). Cheltenham: Edward Elgar.

Deloitte (2016). *The Deloitte Millennial survey: Winning over the next generation of leaders.* Retrieved from www2.deloitte.com/content/dam/Deloitte/global/Documents/About-Deloitte/gx-millenial-survey-2016-exec-summary.pdf.

Dols J., Landrum P., & Weick K.L. (2010). Leading and managing an intergenerational workforce. *Creative Nursing,* 16(2), 1–8.

Erickson, T. (2008). *Plugged in: The Generation Y guide to thriving at work.* Boston, MA: Harvard Business School.

Garcia, O. (2013). *The driven organization and what we need to be happy and productive at work.* Troy, MI: Future Approved Works.

Helvey, K. (2016). Don't underestimate the power of lateral career moves for professional growth. *Harvard Business Review* (May 10). Retrieved from https://hbr.org/2016/05/dont-underestimate-the-power-of-lateral-career-moves-for-professional-growth

Hess, N., & Jepsen, D.M. (2009). Career stage and generational differences in the psychological contract. *Career Development International*, 14(3), 261–283.

Hobart, J.W., & Sendek, H. (2014). *Gen Y now: Millennials and the evolution of leadership.* 2nd ed. San Francisco, CA: Wiley & Sons.

Horwitz, F., Heng, C., Quazi, H. A., Nonkwelo, C., Roditi, D., & van Eck, P. (2006). Human resource strategies for managing knowledge workers: an Afro-Asian comparative analysis. *The International Journal of Human Resource Management*, 17(5), 775–811.

Horwitz, F.M. (2013). An analysis of skills development in a transitional economy: the case of the South African labour market. *The International Journal of Human Resource Management,* 24(12), 2435–2451.

Howe, N., & Strauss, W. (2000). *Millennials rising: the next great generation.* New York, NY: Vintage.

Hurst, J., & Good, L. (2009). Generation Y and career choice: The impact of retail career perceptions, expectations and entitlement perceptions. *Career Development International,* 14(6), 570–593.

Kane-Berman, J. (2015). *Born free but still in chains: South Africa's first post-apartheid generation.* South African Institute of Race Relations. Retrieved from http://irr.org.za/reports-and-publications/occasional-reports/files/irr-report-2013-born-free-but-still-in-chains-april-2015.pdf

Kim, H., Knight, D.K., & Crutsinger, C. (2008). Generation Y employees' retail work experience: The mediating effect of job characteristics. *Journal of Business Research,* 62, 548–556.

Kupperschmidt, B. (2000). Multi-generation employees: Strategies for effective management. *Health Care Manager*, 19(1), 65–76.

Lepeley, M.T. (2017). Human Centered Management. The 5 Pillars of Organizational Quality and Global Sustainability. Abingdon, UK: Routledge.

Lloyd, S., Roodt, G., & Odendaal, A. (2011). Critical elements in defining work-based identity in post-Apartheid South Africa. *South African Journal of Industrial Psychology*, 37(1), 1–15.

Lyons, S., Duxbury, L., & Higgins, C. (2005). Are gender differences in basic human values a generational phenomenon? *Sex Roles*, 53(9/10), 763–778.

Malila, V. (2015). Being a Born Free: The misunderstandings and missed opportunities facing young South Africans. *Rhodes Journalism Review* (35), 127–135.

Maphunye, K.J., Ledwaba, M.L., & Kobjana, M.K. (2014). Democracy without accountability, or accountability without democracy? 'Born-free' perspectives of public representatives in South Africa. *Journal of Public Administration*, 49(1), 161–179.

Markova, G., & Ford, C. (2011). Is money the panacea? Rewards for knowledge workers. *International Journal of Productivity and Performance Management*, 60(8), 813–823.

Martin, C. (2005). From high maintenance to high productivity: What managers need to know about Generation Y. *Industrial and Commercial Training,* 37(1), 39–44.

Martins, N. & Martins, E.C. (2010). Assessing Millennials in the South African work context. In Ng, E., Lyons, S., & Schweitzer, L. (Eds.), *Managing the New Workforce* (pp. 152–177). Cheltenham, UK: Edward Elgar.

Mattes, R. (2011). The "Born Frees": The prospects for generational change in post-apartheid South Africa. *AfroBarometer Working Paper No. 131.* Retrieved from http://afrobarometer.org/sites/default/files/publications/Working%20paper/Afropaper No131.pdf

Mbigi, L. (2000). *In search of the African business renaissance: An African cultural perspective.* Johannesburg: Knowledge Resources.

McKechnie, I., & Bridgens, S. (2008). Engineering skills – key to effective service delivery in South Africa's electricity distribution sector. In *2008 Electricity Distribution Maintenance Summit* (pp. 1–9). Johannesburg: South African Institute of Electrical Engineers (SAIEE).

Meister, J.C., & Willyerd, K. (2010). Mentoring millennials. *Harvard Business Review*, 88(5), 1–5.

Metcalf, O. (2011). *Motivation of technical knowledge workers in a high-tech development environment.* Unpublished Master's thesis. University of Cape Town.

Moroko, L., & Uncles, M. (2008), Characteristics of successful employer brands, *Journal of Brand Management,* 16 (3), 160–175.

Moye, J. (2013). *Hire power: How social media is changing the way people search for jobs.* Retrieved from www.coca-colacompany.com/stories/hire-power-how-social-media-is-changing-the-way-people-search-for-jobs

Mula, A. (2014). *The impact of employment equity legislation on employee engagement within Generation Y.* Unpublished Master's thesis. University of Pretoria.

Ng, E.S.W., Schweitzer, L., & Lyons, S.T. (2010). New generation, great expectations: A field study of the millennial generation. *Journal of Business and Psychology*, 25, 281–292.

Ng, T.W.H., & Feldman, D.C. (2010). Idiosyncratic deals and organizational commitment. *Journal of Vocational Behavior*, 76(3), 419–427.

Parry, E., Unite, J., Chudzikowski, K., Briscoe, J., & Shen, Y. (2010). Career success in the younger generation. In Ng, E., Lyons, S., & Schweitzer, L. (Eds.), *Managing the New Workforce* (pp. 242–261). Cheltenham: Edward Elgar.

Rasch, R., & Kowske, B. (2010). Will Millennials save the world through work? International generational differences in the relative importance of corporate social responsibility and business ethics to turnover intentions. In Ng, E., Lyons, S., & Schweitzer, L. (Eds.), *Managing the New Workforce* (pp. 222–241). Cheltenham, UK: Edward Elgar.

Republic of South Africa (1998). *Employment Equity Act, No.55.* Pretoria: Government Printer.

Ronnie, L., & Wakeling, P. (2015). Motivations and challenges: The South African Masters in Business Administration (MBA) Experience. *International Journal of Teaching and Education,* 3(1), 45–63.

Rousseau, D.M, Hornung, S., & Tai, G.K. (2009). Idiosyncratic deal: testing propositions on timing, content, and the employment relationship [Electronic Version]. *Journal of Vocational Behavior,* 74(3), 338–348.

Rousseau, D.M. (2001). The idiosyncratic deal: Flexibility versus fairness? *Organisational Dynamics,* 29(4), 260–273.

Shandler, D. (2009). *Motivating the millennial knowledge worker: Help today's workforce succeed in today's economy.* Seattle, WA: Crisp.

Shaw, S., & Fairhurst, D. (2008). Engaging a new generation of graduates. *Education and Training,* 50(5), 366–378.

Shrivastavaa, S., Selvarajaha, C., Meyerb, D., & Dorasamy, N. (2014). Exploring excellence in leadership perceptions amongst South African managers. *Human Resource Development International,* 17(1), 47–66.

Smola, K., & Sutton, C. (2002). Generational differences: Revisiting generational work values for the new millennium. *Journal of Organizational Behavior,* 23(4), 363–382.

South African National Treasury (2015). *Provincial budgets and expenditure review: 2010/11–2016/17.* Retrieved from www.treasury.gov.za/publications/igfr/2015/prov/03.%20Chapter%203%20-%20Education.pdf

Tapscott, D. (2009). *Grown up digital: How the Net Generation is changing your world.* New York, NY: McGraw-Hill.

Terjesen, S., & Frey, R-V. (2008). Attracting and retaining Generation Y knowledge worker talent. In Vaiman, V., and Vance, C.M. (Eds.), *Smart Talent Management: Building Knowledge Assets for Competitive Advantage* (pp. 66–92). Northampton, MA: Edward Elgar.

Thompson, C., & Gregory, J. B. (2012). Managing millennials: A framework for improving attraction, motivation, and retention. *The Psychologist-Manager Journal,* 15(4), 237–246.

Thompson, L., & Aspinwall, K. (2009). The recruitment value of work/life benefits. *Personnel Review,* 38(2), 195–210.

Todericiu, R., Şerban, A., & Dumitraşcu, O. (2013). Particularities of knowledge workers' motivation strategies in Romanian organizations. *Procedia Economics and Finance,* 6(13), 405–413.

Tutu, D. (2000). *No future without forgiveness.* Johannesburg: Rider Books.

Van der Walt, S., & Du Plessis, T. (2010). Leveraging multi-generational workforce values in interactive information societies. *South African Journal of Information Management,* 12(1).

Weick, K.L. (2003). Faculty for the millennium: Changes needed to attract the emerging workforce into nursing. *Journal of Nursing Education,* 42, 151–160.

Weick, K.L., Prydun, M., & Walsh, T. (2002). What the emerging workforce wants in its leaders. *Journal of Nursing Scholarship,* 34(3), 283–288.

Wiedmer, T. (2015). Generations do differ: Best practices in leading Traditionalists, Boomers, and Generations X, Y, and Z. *Delta Kappa Gamma Bulletin,* 82(1), 51–58.

Wilson B., Squires M., Widger K., Cranley L., & Tourangeau A. (2008). Job satisfaction among a multigenerational nursing workforce. *Journal of Nursing Management,* 16, 716–723.

Zemke, R., Raines, C., & Filipczak, B. (2000). *Generations at work: Managing the clash of Veterans, Boomers, Xers and Nexters in your workplace,* 2nd ed. New York, NY: Amacom.

10 Exploring education for wellbeing in Peru

Kety Jáuregui

Introduction

Education is a critical element of development to attain human wellbeing. Yet government-formulated policies based exclusively on economic growth formulas are receiving increasing criticism as an explanatory factor for development due to growing evidence that these policies do not show a directly positive effect on poverty reduction, as the trickle-down theory predicts (Aghion & Bolton, 1997), unless a redistributive policy is implemented in parallel (Kakwani & Pernia, 2000).

In this context "growth" alludes to economic expansion of per capita GDP but it does not show if people are reaching a state of wellbeing (Sen, 1988) inherent to all human pursuits. In contrast "development" refers to people's quality of life and continuous improvement associated with a specific outcome. The concept of development, known as "sustainable development," includes economic, social, and environmental dimensions, with the goal to fulfil the needs of current generations without adversely affecting future generations (United Nations Educational, Scientific and Cultural Organization [UNESCO], 2014a). In sustainable development wellbeing is a fundamental indicator along with the pursuit of happiness as a universal aspiration (United Nations [UN], 2011).

UNESCO (2014c) posits that to create a sustainable world, people and societies should be equipped with knowledge, competencies, and values that train them and empower them to follow the sustainable road. In turn, people and societies should be responsible and ready to carry out needed changes to achieve sustainability. According to Lepeley, the quality of education is the platform par excellence to generate and transmit knowledge, competencies, and values that foster people's holistic development, reducing vulnerability and increasing resilience for achievement of wellbeing and a better future (Lepeley, 2017a).

The objective of this chapter is to discuss the importance of education to attain wellbeing and sustainability as fundamental elements of sustainable development. First, the relationship between sustainable development and wellbeing will be analyzed; second, how education relates to sustainable development; and finally, how aspects of Peruvian education relate to sustainability are identified.

Sustainable development and wellbeing

Sustainability is a broad concept, open to multiple interpretations. It is complex, still under construction and associated with social, economic, ethical, cultural, and spiritual dimensions (Wals & Jickling, 2002). It is considered as a paradigm to conceptualize the future where social, economic, and environmental considerations are balanced in the search for a better quality of life for people and society.

The difference between sustainability and sustainable development lies in the fact that sustainability is a long-term goal, while sustainable development is commonly understood as a set of proposals that may, or may not, lead to long-term sustainability. These proposals are frequently related to processes and strategies such as sustainable agriculture, sustainable production, sustainable consumption, good governance, education, and capacity development (UNESCO, 2015).

The Organization for Economic Co-operation and Development [OECD] (2016) indicates that health, education, and employment are the most critical factors associated with wellbeing. University-educated people tend to show higher levels of satisfaction with life than those with school-level education (OECD, 2016). In this sense, Sen (1998) indicates that the development of human capacities has a direct impact on wellbeing.

The perception of happiness is a subjective feeling of wellbeing backed up by individual and sociocultural aspects (Yamamoto, 2013). Helliwell *et al.* (2017) hold that wellbeing / happiness is the best indicator of human development, social progress, and sustainable development and it is increasingly considered as an objective in public policy.

Moreover, in the sustainable development agenda put forth by the United Nations (2011), the pursuit of happiness is called a fundamental human goal and a universal aspiration. The creation of a new economic paradigm is sought aiming to achieve lifelong human happiness and wellbeing, starting with: ecological sustainability; equitable distribution of resources; efficient use of resources; to attain human, social, and cultural prosperity (Royal Government of Bhutan, 2012; Sachs, 2016).

Additionally the concept of "happiness" has been broadened to sustainable happiness that contributes to individual, community-wide, and global wellbeing without exploiting other people or the environment and without affecting future generations (O'Brien, 2016). This conceptualization of happiness may contribute to the development of a unified vision that fosters wellbeing for all and forever (Hopkins, 2013).

Some indicators that show the importance of the pursuit of happiness and wellbeing in development are Gross National Happiness [GNH] (Royal Government of Bhutan, 2012); the Global Competitiveness Index [GCI] produced by the World Economic Forum, which aims to capture the ability of each country to generate good jobs and high incomes for the population; the SDG Index [SDGI] published in the World Happiness Report as part of the UN Sustainable

Development Solutions Network [SDSN], which follows the progress of the 17 Sustainable Development Objectives [SDO] in countries worldwide; and WIN/Gallup International's Global Barometer of Hope and Happiness.

However, it is important to note a controversy that exists on these indices because they measure different components of development. For example, some specialists indicate that the evaluation of wellbeing should include only aspects related to ecological diversity and resilience (NDP Steering Committee and Secretariat, 2013). Meanwhile others, such as Lepeley (2017a), point out the importance of complementing the conventional GDP and macroeconomic considerations leading to optimal employment ratios with advanced formulas of human development anchored in quality education for all to optimize technology and environmental care, as necessary conditions to attain human centered sustainability.

In this sense, studies show that economic competitiveness [GCI] and the Sustainable Development Objectives expressed in the SDG Index, complemented by national per capita income and high employment rates, would provide a better understanding of the conditions associated with wellbeing and happiness (Sachs, 2016).

Education and sustainable development

Education is the most important factor for sustainable development. The development of people's abilities allows them to make more responsible and well-grounded decisions at the individual and collective levels, helping them to face present and future social, economic, and environmental challenges (UNESCO, 2012), and to build more inclusive societies (UNESCO, 2008).

Scope and value

Individual level

Education is essential to developing full potential in life, optimizing holistic development, integrating intelligence, sensitivity, and spirituality; increasing resilience; strengthening independence and critical thinking; and reducing vulnerabilities to attain a better future (Lepeley, 2017a). Likewise, education fosters citizens' self-confidence, tolerance, proactivity, and capacity to integrate values, attitudes, knowledge, and competencies (Office of International Education [OIE], 2017).

Collective level

Education fosters productivity and social cohesiveness, and contributes to decrease poverty (Pârgaru *et al.*, 2009; United Nations Development Programme [UNDP], 2016), more educated people have higher participation in the workforce and have higher level of income (Canton, 2007; Pârgaru *et al.*, 2009), tend to create more harmonious work environment, reduce national unemployment, and achieve a higher level of social development (Pârgaru *et al.*, 2009). Higher levels of education provide people with the knowledge and skills necessary to become active participants in society and social protagonists (Pârgaru, 2015).

Integrating all levels

Education for sustainable development [ESD] aims on educating to foster sustainable societies (UNESCO, 2012). In essence it implies a discussion of the destiny of humanity including roles and responsibilities (Wals & Jickling, 2002). This education paradigm is founded on the belief that people should learn to know, learn to do, learn to live with others, learn to be, and learn to be transformed in order to transform society (UNESCO, 2012), placing humans as the center of sustainable development (UNESCO, 2017a) in such a way that increased human capital people can help people to pursue individual goals in sync with collective wellbeing, building the fundamental stages of inclusive societies worldwide (Sen 1988; Lepeley, 2002, 2017b).

On the same token, the Office of International Education (2017) holds that ESD means: first, transforming the lives of individuals and communities through education as an essential agent of change; second, having a holistic vision of development, recognizing its multi-dimensionality with regard to sustainability, inclusion, social justice, equity, and cohesion; third, acting from a humanistic perspective based on values, attitudes, and behaviors that create and foment dignity, respect, and healthy coexistence with others; fourth, trusting in the power of education to increase wellbeing and the life opportunities available to people and communities; and finally, thinking of and managing development as the convergence of cultural, political, economic, and social components, emphasizing the role of education and the responsibility of educators to bring them all together (OIE, 2017).

Due to the importance of education for human beings, governments are implementing policies to transform education to fit with the new models and objectives of the twenty-first century. Initiatives range from health promoting school programs, social and emotional learning, and entrepreneurship education (O'Brien, 2013, 2016), to proposals for sustainable wellbeing (Hopkins, 2013).

Indeed, educating for sustainability implies integrating and re-orienting diverse disciplines and areas of knowledge linked to education, making them converge in order to synchronize individual and collective goals.

Moreover, educating for sustainability also implies that the increase of human capital is valuable and desirable but not as an end unto itself. To focus on education on human capital alone could be a utilitarian perspective of human beings, considering them as mere instruments of production. In contrast, a human centered education seeks the continuous improvement of the human talent that contributes to the development of human capital. Likewise, ESD should permit people to achieve wellbeing for themselves and others.

Mechanisms of ESD

ESD is a broad concept that encompasses all aspects of sustainability, from environmental to social to economic, along with the underlying dimension of culture as well as education in management including planning, policies, programs, financing, curricula, teaching and learning, and evaluations.

UNESCO (2012) emphasizes the alignment in the following areas to attain sustainability: improvement in access to (enrollment) and retention to school education; educational programs reoriented in sustainability; and continuous training for all sectors of the labor force. These needs are critical to make decisions aimed at sustainability. These core concepts originate from Chapter 36 of "Agenda 21" – the agreement signed by UN member nations to promote sustainable development, approved at the United Nations Conference on Environment and Development (UNCED) held in Rio de Janeiro in 1992 (UN, 1992).

Access and retention at school level

The priority of ESD is to facilitate access to education at pre-school, primary, and secondary levels, and fundamentally to improve education quality. Because, on one hand, the hurdle of self-education is a problem that affects large sectors of the population at the global level, and especially girls and illiterate adults; and on the other hand, a large proportion of children worldwide only has access to low levels of education, which creates a significant obstacle to achieve sustainability for individuals and nations.

However, expanding education coverage is not enough: ensuring that students stay in school is a critical issue, as dropping out hinders opportunities to enter the workforce and to be able to meet the demands of the economy and society (UNESCO, 2006).

The United Nations outlined several goals on this matter: universal access to school education, so that at least 80 percent of school-aged children finish school-level education; reduction of the illiteracy rate among adults; and reduction of gender gap in school completion and in illiteracy rate (UN, 1992). It is important to mention that these central concepts do not appear in the Agenda 21 but are underlying ideas reorienting education toward sustainable development (UN, 1992).

Reorientation of educational programs toward sustainability

A more sustainable future cannot be achieved by just providing more access to education (UNESCO, 2006) or increasing coverage. The content and relevance of what is taught to students must be continuously improved. Consequently it is important to question, reconsider, and revise educational programs in order to include more principles, knowledge, competencies, focuses, and values related to sustainability in each area related to environment, society, and the economy, starting at preschool level and following through to university education (UNESCO, 2006).

The reorientation of educational programs implies that sustainability must be included the curriculum and aptitudes, such as critical thinking, organization, and interpretation of data and information, and the capacity to formulate questions – all must be developed in the educational context (UN, 2006).

Education needs to be closely related to developmental issues and the environment, linked to social education and integration of ecological concepts (demography and analysis of the causes of main environmental and developmental problems), taking into account unique local contexts (UN, 1992).

Training the labor force to make sustainable decisions

Access to education and lifelong learning for the continuous development of relevant capacities are critical factors in improving students' rate of employability and crucial to synchronizing labor supply and demand, and, by extension, sustainability. It is also necessary to bear in mind that rapid technological change, especially automation and robotics, are increasingly affecting jobs and employment (OECD, Economic Commission for Latin America and the Caribbean [ECLAC] & Development Bank of Latin America [CAF], 2015).

Organizational advantages are closely linked to human capital, talent management, organizational resilience, agility, quality standards, and the challenges associated with an adequate level of education to meet demands for productivity and sustainability (Lepeley, 2017b). Sadly, and primarily, although not necessary a problem for developing countries, the level of education many workers reach is below labor market demands. It is estimated that 35 percent of global human capital potential is not properly developed due to deficient educational systems that fail to meet employment opportunities (World Economic Forum [WEF], 2016a).

The central role of education takes into account that, in addition to offering knowledge that permits people access to jobs and employment, it also informs about the relationship between the environment and sustainable development (UN, 1992).

The Peruvian Case

Peru has a population of 31,826 (Compañía Peruana de Estudios de Mercado y Opinión Pública [CPI], 2017), largely shaped by mestizos, while two-thirds is urban. In terms of population Peru is the fifth most populous country in South America (United Nations Development Program [UNDP.PERU], 2017). It has a territorial surface of 1,285,215.60 km^2 (Instituto Nacional de Estadística e Informática [INEI], 2013). According to the UN Peru is one of the ten most megadiverse countries in the world with a wide diversity of resources (UNDP. PERU, 2017). Its current system of government is organized under the principle of separation of powers: Executive Power (presidential system democratically elected), Legislative Power (exercised by the Congress of the Republic), and Judicial Power (UNDP.PERU, 2017). Its rate of economic growth in the last decades has been one of its greatest achievements, allowing increasing macro-economic stability, and reduced inflation, external debt, and poverty (UNDP. PERU, 2017). In 2016 UN includes Peru among the human development countries, ranking 87 of 188 countries with a score of 0.74 (UNDP, 2016). Between 2005 and 2015 the labor force participation rate increased from 71.1 percent to 71.6 percent (Ministerio de Trabajo y Promoción del Empleo [MTPE], 2016).

As one of the ten most diverse countries in Latin America, Peru plays a key role in the ecological equilibrium of the world (UNDP, 2016).

The Peruvian educational system has compulsory school education and higher education. Compulsory education lasts twelve years including one year of preschool education, six years of primary school, and five years of secondary school.

Higher education is delivered in two dimension s: (a) university education, offered by universities granting academic university degrees that commonly last for a minimum of five years; and (b) technical education, offered by technical schools granting technical degrees that vary in extension between six months and three years. Starting in 2017 students can earn technical school credits that they can transfer to pursue studies in universities (Ministry of Education [MINEDU], 2017).

Mechanisms to advance towards sustainability through education

The central concepts for ESD put forth by UNESCO (2012) deal with three important mechanisms that can help the Peruvian education system have a greater impact on sustainability.

Access to and retention of school education

In Peru, public education is universal and free of charge. Compulsory education enrollments have steadily increased in preschools and secondary schools, but not in primary level. At preschool level, the net rate of enrolled of children between ages three and five was 83.2 percent in 2015, showing a 5.9 percent increase over three years (Estadística de la Calidad Educativa [ESCALE], 2016d). For secondary education, net rate of enrollment for students between the ages of 12 and 16 increased 13.5 percent between 2005 and 2011 (Instituto Nacional de Estadística e Informática [INEI], 2016c).

The Ministry of Education [MINEDU] (2017) recently carried out educational reforms, starting with an evaluation program of public school teachers with the purpose to train them and offer students education that meets quality standards focused on students' needs and based on improved working conditions.

Additionally, MINEDU worked to improve learning programs, offering pedagogical support to teachers at primary level and increasing training in mathematics and science to extend school time and create the Full School Day at the secondary level (MINEDU, 2014).

Likewise, policies to improve school management with programs targeting the selection of principals and assistant principals have been implemented (OECD, 2016). With regard to infrastructure, laws have been enacted to encourage private investment through programs such as public–private partnerships and "Works for Taxes" in order to improve institutional infrastructure.

Despite efforts carried out by the government, universal enrollment of children and teenagers schooling has not been accomplished, and neither have the expected educational results. There is a substantial number of areas of improvement necessary to achieve the sustainable development target in education – among others, increased enrollment of children between six and 11 years of age in grade levels that correspond to their age group. In primary education, the net rate of school enrollment for six to 11 year olds decreased from 92.6 percent in 2005 to 91.4 percent in 2015 (Instituto Nacional de Estadística e Informática [INEI], 2016a).

Additionally, the Human Capital Report (World Economic Forum [WEF], 2016a) shows that, for the 0–14 age group, Peru is in 81st place among 130 countries in primary school enrollment (WEF, 2016b). Therefore, the government needs to design integral strategies to enroll children in this age cohort, given that primary school is one of most significant educational levels to advance human development.

Furthermore, the percentage of students who complete secondary education is 82 percent, well below the 94 percent average among OECD countries (OECD, Economic Commission for Latin America and the Caribbean [ECLAC] & Development Bank of Latin America [CAF], 2016).

It is also important to improve access strategies for children in rural areas to bridge significant gaps between urban and rural education (INEI, 2016c). In 2015 14.8 percent of the rural population 15 years and older was illiterate, 4.5 times higher than the urban rate of illiteracy (3.2 percent) (INEI, 2016c).

It is important to increase public investment in education, aiming to improve infrastructure and teacher training. In 2015 Peru's investment in education reached 3.6 percent of GDP (ESCALE, 2016a), well below the Latin American average, which in 2014 was 4.6 percent of GDP (UNESCO, 2014b).

In 2016 39.2 percent of Peruvian public schools had no connection to electric power. Less than 46 percent had access to drinkable water, and 49.4 percent had no sewer connection (ESCALE, 2016b). With regard to teacher academic profiles of teachers, in 2013, 55 percent of secondary school teachers and 45.7 percent of primary school teachers had university degrees (Espinoza *et al.*, 2015). It is predicted that by 2021 Peru will have a deficit of 94,463 primary education teachers and 38,405 secondary education teachers (Espinoza *et al.*, 2015).

These statistics explain that, since 2000, Peruvian students have scored among the lowest in Latin America and the world in PISA (Programme for International Student Assessment) test (MINEDU, 2016b; OCDE, 2016; Ganimian, 2016). Peru ranked 129th in quality of primary education in the Global Competitiveness Index (WEF, 2017). In 2015, the Census of Student Evaluation showed that 15 percent of Peruvian students in the second year of secondary school achieved a satisfactory level in reading comprehension and 10 percent in mathematics (MINEDU, 2016b).

Reorientation of educational programs toward sustainability

Despite the above results Peru has carried out several programs to improve the development of knowledge and abilities the students require to promote sustainable development. In 2016, the new National Curriculum of Basic Education [CNEB], which moved from a content-centered model to a competency-based model, was approved (MINEDU, 2016a). The objectives of the CNEB (2016) are aligned with UNESCO's 2030 Agenda (2017), based on the ethical, spiritual, cognitive, emotional, communicative, physical, environmental, cultural, and socio-political development of students to advance towards integral training for personal development and exercise of citizenship for holistic fulfillment. This program includes learning goals oriented to collectively build democracy for national development (MINEDU, 2016a).

These educational programs need to be strengthened to attain sustainability – for example, including topics linked to sustainability, biodiversity, climate change, and equity to discuss the local and national challenges for sustainability (UNESCO, 2012).

Another aspect of education that is important in attaining sustainability is to focus education on inclusiveness – that is, placing attention on distinctive features of students and avoiding categorizations that divide them (UNESCO, 2017b). Peruvian education at primary level is provided to teenagers and adults who have not completed regular primary level, and for gifted students and children and is differentiated by groups (MINEDU, 2012).

Training of the labor force for sustainable decision-making

The percentage of Peruvians over the age of 15 enrolled in higher education has increased faster among students who enroll in universities (from 12 percent to 14 percent between 1997 and 2015) in comparison with students who attend lower level of higher education (7 percent to 12.5 percent) (INEI, 2016a; Síntesis Estadística, 2016).

Besides, Peru is taking actions to facilitate the insertion of people who have completed higher education into the workforce, developing work training programs and employment by generation programs that are managed by the Ministry of Labor and Employment Promotion [MTPE] to promote the development of technical knowledge among people with low skills from low-income households.

Additionally, Peru has developed important private initiatives to improve labor force skills, creating private educational institutions associated with large industrial and financial business groups investing in education to counteract the results of public educational institutions that fail to train students in skills needed in the workforce. Initiatives of the private sector include a fast expansion of programs in corporate social responsibility aimed to help community improvement, offering scholarships to students, development programs for students and teachers, training programs to develop skills of young people and work techniques, and opening options for the sponsoring companies to hire the best participants. Most of these programs are directed to support students who have finished secondary school, giving them access to integrate the workforce.

In spite of all the public and private initiatives to aid improvement of the workforce, there is still a deficit of people with in technical school education and skills and qualified labor in rural areas (INEI, 2016c). This is a shortcoming that hinders progress in the productive sector in rural regions and negatively impacts sustainability. This opens the opportunity for improvement centered on creating more technical schools in rural areas, because at the present time only 2.4 percent of Peruvian technical schools are located in rural areas, and 1 percent of the students enrolled in technical education are from rural areas (ESCALE, 2016c).

Another opportunity for improvement in higher education would be to promote the study of new majors, because now over 50 percent of the students enroll in traditional majors (education, law, and business administration) and avoid technical majors that are necessary for development and sustainability (INEI, 2016c). Overall it is important to focus attention on encouraging students to complete technical and university educational programs because today close to 15 percent graduate from those programs (ESCALE, 2016c; INEI, 2016b) and fewer than 10 percent graduate university studies (INEI, 2016c; INEI, 2015).

At the same time, the development of certain abilities, especially soft skills and a better and broader understanding of sustainability, have not received high priority in any sector of the Peruvian educational system. This is in spite of the fact that soft skills have been in increasing demand in quality organizations worldwide (Lepeley & Albornoz, 2013), showing opportunity for the improvement of the curricula in both universities and technical schools, and the need to develop workshops to develop these skills in professional organizations and businesses.

Peru is lagging behind on the need to better synchronize education and training with demands of the workforce.

To sum up, the main problems the Peruvian labor market faces today are, first, public sector ignorance of labor demands in the business sector, and, second, the disconnect between labor market demands and levels of education and the competencies workers need to in order to perform well at work.

High performance at work, in turn, results in higher wages, a higher quality of life, and increasing wellbeing, which are all necessary to meet personal and family needs to achieve a better life. Moreover, the 2017 edition of the Global Competitiveness Report shows that Peru had fallen five places in this competitiveness index, to 72nd place out of 137 countries and in 124th place on the quality of higher education and training (WEF, 2017).

Wellbeing

According to numerous statistics, Latin America is the happiest region in the world, but Peru is second-to-last place among the seven Latin American countries included in a study. Peru shows a net happiness index of 61 percent, which is above the average global happiness index, and is positioned in 22nd place among 66 countries (Vega & King, 2016). These findings coincide with the results of the World Happiness Report 2017, in which Peru came 14th out of 18 countries in the Region, eighth out of ten for South America, and 63rd out of 155 countries worldwide (Helliwell *et al.*, 2017). It is apparent that in Peru the sense of wellbeing has improved in recent years due mainly to an increased perception of social support from networks of family and friends (Helliwell *et al.*, 2017).

Conclusions

Peru has advanced with regard to the access of children and teenagers to school education. It has re-formulated school curriculum, incorporating a human development focus centered on learning over teaching. Some of these programs have been developed with support from the public and private sector aiming to better prepare the workforce. Furthermore, attention and effort have been given to improve the normative framework of management in higher education. But this framework has not yet been able to generate and deliver effective ESD (education for sustainable development). In spite of good intentions, successful efforts are isolated and little attention is given to fundamental issues, such as the environment and bridging urban–rural gaps. Therefore significant impact on wellbeing and increased happiness has not been attained. Although Peru seems to be in a better position to reduce unhappiness, more effective development strategies on education are required to attain wellbeing.

Education is the main drive to advance sustainable development, reduce human vulnerabilities, and to empower responsible people in the fulfillment of human needs and to improve the condition of current generations without negative effects on future generations. This is a fundamental condition for sustainability education to advance to sustainable development.

Wellbeing is a critically important measurement of progress and sustainable development considered a most relevant and increasingly objective indicator for governments and decision-makers. Wellbeing is reflected in the perception of happiness. To the extent that it consolidates the importance of human happiness, it is the best predictor of long-term sustainability at individual and social levels of prosperity.

ESD is relevant at the individual level but crucial at collective level, because it contributes to uniting – instead of dividing – people as it induces higher participation that fosters the positive social change required to support the development of sustainable societies.

Peru has been growing in macroeconomic terms, and this has allowed for important economic stability, but economic growth alone does not lead to sustainability and socially oriented actions, especially focused on the positive effects of education for sustainable development are required (Lepeley, 2017a).

References

Aghion, P., & Bolton, P. (1997). A Theory of Trickle-Down Growth and Development. *The Review of Economic Studies*, 64(2), 151–172.

Banco de Desarrollo de América Latina [CAF]. (2015). *Educación técnica y profesional en Perú*. Retrieved from http://scioteca.caf.com/bitstream/handle/123456789/826/ETFP% 20Per%C3%BA%20Final%205.pdf?sequence=1&isAllowed=y

Canton, E. (2007). Social returns to education: Macro-evidence. *Economist*, 155(4), 449–468. Retrieved from http://link.springer.com/article/10.1007/s10645-007-9072-z

Compañía Peruana de Estudios de Mercado y Opinión Pública [CPI] (2017). *Market Report*. Retrieved from:

Espinoza, E., Espezua, L., & Choque, R. (2015). *¿Qué significa ser profesor en el Perú? Evidencia para una política de inversión en el talento*. Programa Nacional de Becas y Crédito Educativo. Retrieved from http://aplicaciones.pronabec.gob.pe/CIIPRE/Content/ descargas/e5.pdf

Estadística de la Calidad Educativa [ESCALE]. (2016a). *Acceso a la educación*. Retrieved from http://escale.minedu.gob.pe/tendencias

Estadística de la Calidad Educativa [ESCALE]. (2016b). *Recursos invertidos en educación*. Retrieved from http://escale.minedu.gob.pe/tendencias

Estadística de la Calidad Educativa [ESCALE]. (2016c). *Entorno de enseñanza*. Retrieved from http://escale.minedu.gob.pe/tendencias

Estadística de la Calidad Educativa [ESCALE]. (2016d). *Magnitudes*. Retrieved from http://escale.minedu.gob.pe/magnitudes

Ganimian, A. (2016). *Bajos resultados, altas mejoras ¿Cómo les fue a los estudiantes peruanos de primaria y secundaria en las últimas evaluaciones internacionales?* UNESCO. Retrieved from http://unesdoc.unesco.org/images/0024/002449/244955S.pdf

Helliwell, J., Layard, R., & Sachs, J. (2017). *World Happiness Report 2017*. Retrieved from http://worldhappiness.report/wp-content/uploads/sites/2/2017/03/HR17.pdf

Hopkins, C. (2013). Educating for Sustainability: An Emerging Purpose of Education. *Kappa Delta Pi Record*, 49(3), 122–125.

http://cpi.pe/images/upload/paginaweb/archivo/26/mr_poblacion_peru_2017.pdf

www.inei.gob.pe/media/MenuRecursivo/publicaciones_digitales/Est/Lib1140/cap01.pdf

Instituto Nacional de Estadística e Informática [INEI] (2013). *Anuario de Estadísticas Ambientales 2013*. Retrieved from:

Instituto Nacional de Estadística e Informática [INEI]. (2015). *Encuesta Nacional a Egresados Universitarios y Universidades*. Retrieved from www.inei.gob.pe/media/Menu Recursivo/publicaciones_digitales/Est/Lib1298/Libro.pdf

Instituto Nacional de Estadística e Informática [INEI]. (2016a). *Clasificador Nacional de Ocupaciones 2015. Documento preliminar*. Retrieved from www.inei.gob.pe/media/ Clasificador_Nacional_de_Ocupaciones_9_de_febrero.pdf

Instituto Nacional de Estadística e Informática [INEI]. (2016b). *Compendio Estadístico: Perú 2016*. Retrieved from www.inei.gob.pe/media/MenuRecursivo/publicaciones_ digitales/Est/Lib1375/cap05/ind05.htm

Instituto Nacional de Estadística e Informática [INEI]. (2016c). *Perú: Indicadores de Educación por Departamentos, 2005–2015*. Retrieved from www.inei.gob.pe/media/ MenuRecursivo/publicaciones_digitales/Est/Lib1360/index.html

Kakwani, N., & Pernia, E. (2000). What is Pro-poor Growth? *Asian Development Review*, 18(1), 1–16.

Lepeley, M. (2002). Gestión de Calidad en educación superior: Condición para maximizar el beneficio de la globalización. *Pensamiento Educativo*, 31, 203–235.

Lepeley, M. (2017a). Bhutan's Gross National Happiness: An Approach to Human Centred Sustainable Development. *South Asian Journal of Human Resources Management*, 4(2), 174–184.

Lepeley, M. (2017b). *Human Centered Management 5 Pillars of Organizational Quality and Global Sustainability.* Abingdon, UK: Routledge.

Lepeley, M., & Albornoz, C. (2013). Advancing People Skills for Twenty-First Century Business Education in Chile. In I. Alon, V. Jones, & J. Mcintyre, *Innovation in Business Education in Emerging Markets* (pp. 27–42). Basingstoke, UK: Palgrave Macmillan.

Ministerio de Educación [MINEDU]. (2012). *Educación Básica Especial y Educación Inclusiva. Balance y Perspectivas.* Retrieved from www.minedu.gob.pe/minedu/ archivos/a/002/05-bibliografia-para-ebe/9-educacion-basica-especial-y-educacion-inclusiva-balance-y-perspectivas.pdf

Ministerio de Educación [MINEDU]. (2014). *Jornada Escolar Completa.* Retrieved from www.minedu.gob.pe/a/006.php

Ministerio de Educación [MINEDU]. (2016a). *Currículo Nacional de la Educación Básica.* Retrieved from www.minedu.gob.pe/curriculo/pdf/curriculo-nacional-2016-2.pdf

Ministerio de Educación [MINEDU]. (2016b). *Escolares peruanos mejoran sus aprendizajes de Ciencia, Matemática y Lectura según evaluación PISA.* Retrieved from www.minedu.gob.pe/n/noticia.php?id=41002

Ministerio de Educación [MINEDU]. (2017). *El Perú en PISA 2015. Informe Nacional de Resultados.* Retrieved from http://umc.minedu.gob.pe/wp-content/uploads/2017/ 04/Libro_PISA.pdf

Ministerio de Trabajo y Promoción del Empleo [MTPE] (2016). *Principales indicadores del mercado laboral 2004- 2015.* Retrieved from www2.trabajo.gob.pe/promocion-del-empleo-y-autoempleo/informacion-del-mercado-de-trabajo/peru-total-por-sexo/

NDP Steering Committee and Secretariat. (2013). *Happiness: Towards a New Development Paradigm. Report of the Kingdom of Bhutan.* Retrieved from www.newdevelopment paradigm.bt/wp-content/uploads/2014/10/HappinessTowardsANewDevelopment Paradigm.pdf

O Brien, C. (2013). Happiness and sustainability together at last! Sustainable happiness. *Canadian Journal of Education*, 36(4), 228–256.

O'Brien, C. (2016). *Education for Sustainable Happiness and Well-Being.* Abingdon, UK: Routledge.

Office of International Education [OIE]. (2017). *15 Claves de Análisis para Apuntalar la Agenda Educativa 2030.* UNESCO. Retrieved from http://unesdoc.unesco.org/ images/0025/002590/259069s.pdf

Organisation for Economic Co-operation and Development [OECD]. (2016). *The path to happiness lies in good health and a good job, the Better Life Index shows.* Retrieved from www.oecd.org/social/the-path-to-happiness-lies-in-good-health-and-a-good-job-the-better-life-index-shows.htm

Organisation for Economic Co-operation and Development [OECD]; Economic Commission for Latin America and the Caribbean [ECLAC]; Corporación Andina de Fomento [CAF]. (2015). *Perspectivas económicas de América Latina 2015: Educación, competencias e innovación para el desarrollo.* Retrieved from http://repositorio.cepal. org/bitstream/handle/11362/37445/S1420759_es.pdf

Organisation for Economic Co-operation and Development [OECD]; Economic Commission for Latin America and the Caribbean [ECLAC]; Corporación Andina de Fomento

[CAF]. (2016). *Perspectivas económicas de América Latina 2016: Hacia una nueva asociación con China.* Retrieved from http://repositorio.cepal.org/bitstream/handle/11362/39535/S1501061_es.pdf?sequence=1

Pârgaru, I., Gherghina, R., & Duca, I. (2009). The role of education in the knowdelge-based society during the economic crisis. *Annales Universitatis Apulensis Series Oeconomica*, 11(2): 646–651.

Pârgaru, I., Iacob, C., & Iacob, S. (2015). The Interaction of Human Capital with Social Development. *Valahian Journal of Economic Studies*, 6(2), 59–64.

Royal Government of Bhutan. (2012). *The Report of the High-Level Meeting on WellBeing and Happiness: Defining a New Economic Paradigm.* Retrieved from https://sustainable development.un.org/content/documents/617BhutanReport_WEB_F.pdf

Sachs, J. (2016). Happiness and Sustainable Development: Concepts and Evidence. In J. Helliwell, R. Layard, & J. Sachs (Eds.), *World Happiness Report 2016* (p. 56).

Sen, A. (1988). The concept of development. In *Handbook of Development Economics* (pp. 1, 9–26). North Holland: Hollis Chenery and T.N. Srinivasan.

Sen, A. (1998). Capital humano y capacidad humana. *Cuadernos de economía*, 17(29), 67–72.

United Nations Development Program [UNDP.PERU] (2017). *Perú en Breve.* Retrieved from www.pe.undp.org/content/peru/es/home/countryinfo/

United Nations Development Program [UNDP] (2016). *Human Development Reports.* Retrieved from: http://hdr.undp.org/sites/default/files/hdr_2016_report_spanish_web.pdf

United Nations Development Program [UNDP]. (2016). *Informe sobre Desarrollo Humano 2016.* Retrieved from http://hdr.undp.org/sites/default/files/hdr_2016_report_spanish_web.pdf

United Nations Educational, Scientific and Cultural Organization [UNESCO]. (2006). *Decenio de las Naciones Unidas de la Educación con miras al Desarrollo Sostenible (2005–2014) : Plan de aplicación internacional.* Retrieved from http://unesdoc.unesco.org/images/0014/001486/148654so.pdf

United Nations Educational, Scientific and Cultural Organization [UNESCO]. (2008). *Educación para el desarrollo sostenible en la región andina. Algunas experiencias significativas en Ecuador y Venezuela.* Retrieved from http://unesdoc.unesco.org/images/0016/001617/161764s.pdf

United Nations Educational, Scientific and Cultural Organization [UNESCO]. (2012). *Educación para el Desarrollo Sostenible.* Retrieved from http://unesdoc.unesco.org/images/0021/002167/216756s.pdf

United Nations Educational, Scientific and Cultural Organization [UNESCO]. (2014a). *Aichi-Nagoya Declaration on Education for Sustainable Development.* Retrieved from www.unesco.org/fileadmin/MULTIMEDIA/HQ/ERI/pdf/Aichi-Nagoya_Declaration_EN.pdf

United Nations Educational, Scientific and Cultural Organization [UNESCO]. (2014b). *Gasto público en la educación de América Latina ¿Puede servir a los propósitos de la Declaración de París sobre los Recursos Educativos Abiertos?* Retrieved from www.unesco.org/new/fileadmin/MULTIMEDIA/FIELD/Montevideo/pdf/CDCI1-Karisma-ES.pdf

United Nations Educational, Scientific and Cultural Organization [UNESCO]. (2014c). *Hoja de ruta para la implementación del Programa de Acción Mundial sobre Educación para el Desarrollo Sostenible.* Retrieved from http://unesdoc.unesco.org/images/0023/002305/230514s.pdf

United Nations Educational, Scientific and Cultural Organization [UNESCO]. (2015). *Replantear la educación ¿Hacia un bien común mundial?* Retrieved from http://unesdoc. unesco.org/images/0023/002326/232697s.pdf

United Nations Educational, Scientific and Cultural Organization [UNESCO]. (2017a). *UNESCO Global Action Programme on Education for Sustainable development.* Retrieved from http://unesdoc.unesco.org/images/0024/002462/246270e.pdf

United Nations Educational, Scientific and Cultural Organization [UNESCO]. (2017b). *15 Claves de Análisis para apuntalar la Agenda Educativa 2030.* Retrieved from http://unesdoc.unesco.org/images/0025/002590/259069s.pdf

United Nations. (1992). *Cumpre para la tierra. Programa 21.* Departamento de asuntos económicos y sociales. División de desarrollo sostenible. Retrieved from www.un.org/s panish/esa/sustdev/agenda21/agenda21sptoc.htm

United Nations. (2011). *La felicidad: hacia un enfoque holístico del desarrollo.* Retrieved from http://repository.un.org/bitstream/handle/11176/291712/A_RES_65_309-%20ES. pdf?sequence=6&isAllowed=y

Vega, A., & King, Z. (2016). *Barómetro Global de la Esperanza y Felicidad 2016.* Centro Nacional de Consultoría [CNN] and Red WIN/Gallup International. Retrieved from www.cnccol.com/attachments/article/348/CNC_Barometro_2016.pdf

Wals, A. E., & Jickling, B. (2002). "Sustainability" in higher education: From doublethink and newspeak to critical thinking and meaningful learning. *International Journal of Sustainability in Higher Education, 3*(3), 221–232.

World Economic Forum [WEF]. (2016a). *Human Capital Report 2016.* Retrieved from http://reports.weforum.org/human-capital-report-2016/

World Economic Forum [WEF]. (2016b). *The Global Competitiveness Report 2016–2017.* Retrieved from www3.weforum.org/docs/GCR2016–2017/05FullReport/TheGlobal CompetitivenessReport2016–2017_FINAL.pdf

World Economic Forum [WEF]. (2017). *The Global Competitiveness Report 2017.* Retrieved from www3.weforum.org/docs/GCR2017–2018/05FullReport/TheGlobal CompetitivenessReport2017%E2%80%932018.pdf

Yamamoto, J. (2013). Bienestar, gestión de recursos humanos y desarrollo social. *Tiempo de Opinón,* 14–25.

Index

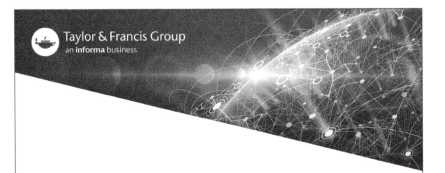

For Product Safety Concerns and Information please contact our EU representative GPSR@taylorandfrancis.com Taylor & Francis Verlag GmbH, Kaufingerstraße 24, 80331 München, Germany

Printed and bound by CPI Group (UK) Ltd, Croydon, CR0 4YY

01/05/2025

01858426-0009